Evaluating Quality Circles in a College of Further Education

Tim Atkinson

Manchester Monographs
The centre for adult and higher education.
University of Manchester

© T. Atkinson

April 1990

ISBN 0 902252 14 3

Printed by: Direct Design (Bournemouth) Ltd., Printers,
3 The Courtyard, Thrush Road, Poole, Dorset, BH12 4NP

CONTENTS

Acknowledgement

Introduction 1

Chapter 1 Quality Circles Background 3

    Quality Circles Background. The Human Relations Movement in Industrial Relations. Organisation Development: Behavioural Science Interventions. Key Quality Circles Concepts. Management of a Quality Circle Programme. Quality Circle Activity. Quality Circles in the U.K. The North American Experience of Quality Circles in Educational Institutions.

Chapter 2 The Introduction of a Quality Circles Programme at Accrington and Rossendale College 31

    Background. Planning and Preparation for a Quality Circle Programme Quality Circle Leader Training. Formation of Quality Circles. Operation of Quality Circles. Problems relating to the operation of Quality Circles. Quality Circle member training, trainer training, and training for Senior Staff in Quality Circle techniques. Presentations/Achievements of Quality Circles. Management and Organisation of the Quality Circle Programme.

Chapter 3 Evaluation of the Programme 45

    Evaluation of the Programme. Benefits anticipated by Opinion Formers. Drawing up of the Questionnaire. The Questionnaire: Final Draft following Piloting. Analysis of the Questionnaire. Interviews with original Opinion Formers and Quality Circle Participants. Commentary by the Consultant. Effects of Quality Circles on Organisational Culture. The future of Quality Circles in the College. The implications of Introducing a Quality Circles Programme for other Colleges. The Extent to which the original Project aims have been achieved. Summary

Bibliography 90

Appendix   Case Study of one Quality Circle's solution to a problem 93

ACKNOWLEDGEMENT

This monograph has only been possible because of funding from the Further Education Unit (FEU) which enabled us to run a Quality Circles programme as a research project at Accrington and Rossendale College between January, 1986 and March, 1987.

Tim Atkinson July 1988

INTRODUCTION

This is not an easy time to be working in FE! Colleges are going through a period of unprecedented pressure and change, some inspired by Central Government, and some caused by demographic change, economic change, and market forces. There are new measures of efficiency and effectiveness, greater financial and managerial autonomy for governing bodies, decline of traditional industrial craft training as the service sector expands, the need to attract new client groups as the number of 16 year olds as a proportion of total population falls. As curriculum changes through the development of competence based learning, open learning, the national reviews of vocational qualifications and "A" levels, and the development of GCSE and pre-vocational education, so learning styles change and the need for staff inservice training increases. Along with growing financial independence there has also been rigorous budgeting and the setting of financial targets, this together with increasing competition from private training agencies has led to pressure on lecturers salaries and conditions of service.

As a result of these trends FE colleges, of which Accrington and Rossendale College is fairly typical, are having to behave increasingly like commercial organisations in the ways that they administer and organise themselves and relate to external agencies. Staff morale has plummeted as they have struggled to come to terms with developing new skills of marketing, consultancy, interpersonal skills, negotiating skills, and so on. A major priority has been the development of management skills amongst senior staff.

Against this background Quality Circles suggested themselves as a way of introducing a participatory management style, increasing staff involvement in the achievement of college aims and objectives, enhancing interpersonal skills, and giving staff a range of problem solving techniques which would be useful in their day to day working lives. The experience of introducing Quality Circles was not without its ups and downs. Many staff, notably support staff joined in with gusto, but a large group of Lecturing staff have remained cynical, reacting with suspicion to what they see as an industrial management trick which should have no place in education.

This monograph seeks to thoroughly consider the Quality Circles experiment at Accrington and Rossendale College by looking at the academic and practical background to circles including their use both in industry in the U.K. and in education both in the U.K. and U.S. There is a description of how they were introduced and developed in the College, and an attempt to evaluate the programme and determine its success. The results were mixed but the experiment was a valuable one.

Tim Atkinson, July 1988.

Chapter 1

QUALITY CIRCLES BACKGROUND

Quality Circles are small volunteer groups of workers who together with a trained leader meet for an hour a week in working time to discuss work problems, investigate causes and recommend solutions to management. Following management approval the Circle implements the solution and moves on to the next problem.

Quality Circles are based on Western ideas of Quality control and Behavioural Science, in particular the theories of McGregor (1966), Herzberg (1968) and Maslow (1970). Following work by Ishikawa (1972) at Tokyo University they were first implemented in Japan as a recognition of the fact that industry was not making full use of the talents and contribution of Japanese workers. The ideas spread rapidly within Japan and abroad and circles now operate in Taiwan, South Korea, Brazil, the U.S.A., and many European countries. Some ten million workers in Japan participate in Circles, fifteen million world-wide. Quality Circle programmes did not begin in Britain until 1978 but their use is growing and the Industrial Society estimates that about 300 firms are involved today.

THE HUMAN RELATIONS MOVEMENT IN INDUSTRIAL RELATIONS

Quality Circles could be considered to be in the mainstream of the human relations movement in industrial relations which has grown over the last 30 years as a reaction to the earlier scientific management movement which saw workers as simply interchangeable parts in a machine who were happy as long as their basic economic and physical needs were met. As a result of this view research in industrial psychology in the 1920s was related to issues such as boredom, fatigue, and the efficient functioning of the human machine. Scientific management theory also regarded the manager as rational and able to control his emotions whereas the worker was irrational, controlled by his emotions and, therefore, inferior to the manager. Freud's ideas, current at the time seemed to support this view. Furthermore, workers were seen as having a limited awareness of themselves and only able to complete tasks requiring a short attention span. A study as early as 1927-32 at the Hawthorne plant of the Western Electric Company began to disprove scientific management theories proving instead that there was no consistent correlation between improvements in the physical environment and productivity of the workforce and that acceptance by fellow workers (the informal organisation) was more important to individuals than economic gain. Argyris (1957) in criticising scientific management theory has pointed out that the theory requires workers to perform with the mentality and motivation of children who he defines as being passive, dependent, and subordinate. He too acknowledges the importance of the informal organisation considering it able to decrease causes of conflict, frustration and failure even though it can be antagonistic to the requirements of the formal organisation.

The human relations movement counters the scientific management view by broadening the concept of the needs and nature of man to include not only the purely physical needs, such as avoidance of hunger, but also emotional and social needs of relating to his fellow workers and realising his own potential by continuous psychological growth. Herzberg (1968) argues that organisations must realise that to use human beings effectively they must be treated in terms of their complete nature rather than in terms of those characteristics which best meet the organisation's needs. His view is that the industrial relations structure in an organisation should comprise two halves, the first dealing with physical and economic needs such as bonus schemes, working conditions, salaries, whereas the second should be concerned with four objectives:

-Training and education for motivation, a mature loyalty to the company based on self fulfilment

-Job enlargement, not just adding new activities but providing real achievement opportunities, working with others to meet challenges

-Remedial or therapeutic actions, to deal with technological obsolescence, poor performance of employees and administrative failure

-Periodic review of company policies and practices to assess their continuing value.

He believes that such a policy would lead to increased creative productivity which would offset total errors caused by freedom given to the individual. However, the new structure would need to pervade the whole organisation including all levels of management.

McGregor (1960) points out that many of the attempts by managers to control behaviour not only raise apprehensions about manipulation and exploitation but are also in direct conflict with human nature and ignore the ingenuity of the average worker which is sufficient to outwit any system of controls devised by management. In practice all relationships in modern industrial organisations involve a high degree of interdependence between workforce and management and excessive reliance on authority creates more problems than it solves. He puts forward two basic and contradictory theories of industrial relations. Theory X reflects a belief that since the average worker dislikes work, has no ambition and simply wants security, he must be directed, controlled and coerced into working towards organisational objectives. McGregor indicates that this has long been the prevailing view but that it is ineffective since it only responds to the workers' basic physical and economic needs, and since these are largely satisfied in modern organisations they are not adequate motivators. Social and emotional needs are ignored by Theory X particularly amongst those at lower levels in the hierarchy and consequently workers become resistant, antagonistic and unco-operative.

Theory Y on the other hand reflects a belief that work is natural to human beings and most are creative and will seek responsibility and show self direction and self control in meeting objectives to which they are committed. However, in modern organisations the intellectual potential of the average human being is only partly used. The challenge for management is to release the enormous potential represented by its workforce. Integration is the central concept whereby members of an organisation can achieve their own goals best by directing their efforts to the success of the enterprise. The main problem here is to harmonise management views about organisational objectives with workers' views about these objectives. Theory Y assumes that people will exercise self direction and self control in the achievement of organisational objectives to the extent that they are committed to those objectives. If the commitment is small then only a slight degree of self direction and self control will be likely and a substantial amount of external influence will be necessary. If it is large many conventional external controls will be superfluous.

Both Herzberg (1968) and McGregor (1960) argue for increased participation by workers in the management of organisations to discuss work related problems and review the effectiveness of work performance. This is seen as being a form of delegation offering major opportunities for ego satisfaction and motivation towards organisational objectives. It is a means of enabling subordinates to discover the satisfaction that comes from tackling problems and finding successful solutions and helping them to realise that they can satisfy their own needs best by working towards organisational objectives.

Theory Y is concerned with the nature of relationships and the creation of an environment which will encourage commitment to organisational objectives and provide opportunities for the maximum exercise of initiative, ingenuity and self direction in achieving them. This is easier said than done since organisations are often rigid and difficult to change. There may be apparently insoluble conflicts between the objectives of the organisation and the satisfaction of individual human needs manifested in apathy, indifference, non involvement, mistrust and conformity. Internal tensions are usually released in harmful ways. Argyris (1970) argues that the causes of deterioration are built into the design of organisational structures and that technology, administrative controls and leadership styles are needed which will lead to organisations being productive, self renewing and effective as well as encouraging personal development amongst each member of the workforce since it is important that the highest aspirations of the workforce should be fulfilled. In particular the developing management information systems must not be used to unilaterally control the workforce but to delegate and give people at lower levels the freedom to make decisions and take on responsibility. Information technology gives the means to control and direct people with great precision. If it is used in this way both workers and some managers will prove negative but creative in finding new ways to beat the system and restore its inefficiency. Argyris (1970 P.40) lists kinds of behaviour associated with interpersonal and technical competence e.g. 'being open to the ideas and feelings of others.' These have a great deal in common with the Quality Circle code of conduct.

ORGANISATION DEVELOPMENT: BEHAVIOURAL SCIENCE INTERVENTIONS

In order to help organisations develop systems which maximise the chances of achieving organisational goals by harmonising these with the goals of individuals for self fulfilment, intervention strategies based on behavioural science have developed in recent years under the heading of organisation development. One definition of this is given by French and Bell (1978 P.14).

> "Organisation Development is a long range effort to improve an organisation's problem solving and renewal processes particularly through a more effective and collaborative management of organisation culture with special emphasis on the culture of formal work teams with the assistance of a change agent or catalyst and the use of the theory and technology of applied behavioural science including action research."

Two fundamental beliefs of an organisation development approach which are consistent with Quality Circle philosophy are that most people have drives towards personal growth and development if provided with an environment that is both supportive and challenging and that most people are capable of contributing more towards organisational objectives than most organisational environments will allow.

Organisation Development is about kinds of organisations, and interventions in the human, social, and cultural systems of the organisation to improve effectiveness. All organisational structures are different, constructed to serve external circumstances. A basic distinction is between organic and mechanistic systems.

Characteristics of a mechanistic system include a high degree of task differentiation and specialisation, a hierarchical management structure with top management controlling both incoming and outgoing communications, vertical interactions between superiors and subordinates, an "informal" social system, a high level of loyalty, both to the organisation and to superiors, a high value placed on knowledge of the workings of the organisation and a one to one leadership style with scant attention paid to group processes. Organic systems are stratified on the basis of expertise with the location of authority determined by consensus. Communications are extensive and open, lateral and diagonal as well as vertical involving people of different rank and across functional groups. Commitment is to the organisation's tasks, progress, and growth rather than to obedience or loyalty. High value is placed on knowing the job, or the context in which the organisation works. The leadership style emphasises interpersonal and group processes.

OD is most suited to organic systems through its emphasis on participation and a collaboratively managed group and organisational structure although some OD efforts can lead to a more mechanistic approach, for example consensus might decide that clearer job descriptions would be a good idea. In general mechanistic systems are suitable to stable conditions, organic systems to changing conditions. No systems are optimal under all conditions, the objective is to find a good mix which optimises the systems relating to technology, tasks, internal and external environments and employee skills. OD must be responsive to this mix rather than merely attempting to impose an organic system.

Harrison (1975) in considering organisational types argues that conflict in the organisational context is caused by organisational culture, but that this is only recognised when the conflict has developed to a point at which it is very difficult to resolve. He gives examples of conflicting organisational cultures, a task oriented culture where it is recognised that everyone has something to contribute to the debate but that decisions once made are adhered to and a power oriented culture with everyone seeking to exert control while impervious to the influence of others. The differences are in fact ideological but are revealed in argument and disruption.

An organisational culture does a number of things. It prescribes relationships and behavioural actions, it specifies goals, values and ways of measuring success, determines the human qualities to be valued, and ways of dealing with external forces. Harrison (1975) goes on to distinguish four clear types of organisation and their relative strengths and weaknesses.

The power orientation type

The power orientation typeis one in which the organisation seeks to dominate its environment with managers exerting power over subordinates, rivalry between peers, and a prevailing determination on growth at any price with people and other organisations as commodities to be exploited. Such an organisation has many flaws, it isn't flexible since all decisions are made at the top, and subordinates tend to distort the message. It will deal well with external threats since there are aggressive people at the top, but because of the internal competition control tends to break down as the organisation becomes large and complex. Motivation levels of "ordinary" people in the organisation are low and far too much energy is used in policing people.

The role orientation type of organisation

The role orientation type of organisation is rational and orderly. Its employees all exhibit predictable behaviour and are responsible and respectable. The structure and operations are slow to adapt to change, and consequently this is not the most effective mode of organisation for concerns operating in free market conditions. It is inflexible owing to its standard operating procedures and too cumbersome to deal with external threats. However it works well without direction from the top because of its well established systems and deals with problems by establishing new rules and procedures.

The task orientation type

All facets of the task orientation model are geared to achieving the goal or target at almost any cost. Power is only respected if it is based on knowledge and competence. This kind of organisation is found in small high risk businesses or in task forces in large firms. It is very good at dealing with complex and changing environments, and copes well with threats owing to good planning and involvement of members at all levels. However there is very little internal cohesion or long term stability and there can be great pressure on those individuals whose specialism declines.

The person orientation organisation

The person orientation organisation exists to serve the needs of its employees. Leadership is by example and there is a great deal of helpfulness, caring, and consensus decision making. The organisation doesn't maximise profits but seeks to provide a reasonable, congenial living for employees. This type of organisation can deal well with change owing to its good communications and fluid structure, but it is less good at dealing with the external environment generally and has difficulty in directing members' activities in unison in the face of an external threat. There is very little internal cohesion.

There is a basic conflict between the interests of people and the interests of organisations and there is no perfect fit between them in any one form of organisational structure, and while there tend to be internal pressures for people orientation types external pressures will always push towards task orientation. An ideal structure might contain elements of many types although this still wouldn't eliminate conflict. One option for the larger organisation is to have its sub units organised in different ways, each with their own culture. Senior managers in addition to directing the business would spend a great deal of time managing conflict.

OD relates to collaboration of all employees in the management of organisational culture, so that organisational goals are met while at the same time individual aspirations and human values are furthered. It is unlikely that this situation will ever be achieved, but a great deal of progress can be made. To remain vital an organisation must respond to problems by tapping the creativity and commitment of all organisation members. In this process both the formal and informal systems which make up the organisation's culture are used. The formal system could be considered to be the policies, procedures, targets, goals, and organisational structure while the informal system relates to perceptions, attitudes, feelings etc. OD capitalises on the strengths of the informal system and makes the formal and informal systems more congruent. In this process the services of a consultant who is not part of the organisation's culture are called upon to help the organisation to solve its problems using a variety of strategies which could be broadly termed action research.

OD interventions are different from traditional interventions since they seek to concentrate on changing and managing the culture of the organisation by using group and organisational processes. Probably the greatest influence in OD has been the laboratory training movement of the 1940s in which behavioural skills exhibited in groups were analysed in controlled conditions. A problem for OD has been to transfer this process to real organisations. Fundamental to OD strategies is the human relations movement belief that people in the work setting want to develop themselves, are able to make a greater contribution, and will respond to a challenging but supportive environment. Since many organisations consist of overlapping work groups with individuals who are members of two or more groups many organisation development interventions are based on developing and improving team building and group processes.

The experience of group work in many organisations involves an atmosphere of boredom, indifference and lack of commitment, unclear objectives, discussion dominated by a few and veering away from the point, lack of listening with the consequent loss of ideas, fear amongst members of looking foolish or a feeling that judgements are being made about them, disagreements suppressed or settled by voting which leaves a truculent minority, actions decided on before all options have been considered, criticism leading to tensions and the hiding of personal feelings. Such a group will avoid discussion of its problems.

The normal organisational means of directing work is a committee which has rigid rules and tends to be frustrating for participants. A committee is only concerned with decision making from a range of options offered. Teams are different, they are task based, they build their own agendas, and set priorities. Members need to become process conscious to play their full part as a team member in keeping the team on course. The team leader must look after the group members, taking note of their feelings and competences, and making sure everyone is able to contribute. The team works to an experiential pattern building reflection, conceptualisation and effectiveness into its processes. Evaluation of its processes and effectiveness in terms of outcomes are critical since these determine how professional the team is in its approach.

McGregor (1960) points out the importance of the face to face group in solving problems of co-ordination and control. Further to this team approaches develop an appreciation of the need for collaboration, are a training ground for skills in problem solving and social interaction, will reduce friction, and lead to unity of purpose without reducing individual motivation. Members of cohesive groups will work at least as hard to achieve group objectives as they will to achieve individual ones. However, many organisations are inept at all levels in accomplishing objectives through group effort, partly through an inadequate understanding of group operations and partly since in a Theory X environment successful group functioning is a threat to management by direction and control. Managers in particular can be poor at collaborating and communicating with those on a similar level (although good at working with subordinates). Generally speaking successful groups involve a relaxed atmosphere, relevant discussion, objectives which are understood and accepted by all members, good listening skills, openness and absence of fears of looking foolish, no suppressed disagreements, decisions reached by consensus, frequent frank and comfortable criticism, all members of the group contributing, and an acceptance of tasks by all members once action is decided on.

The most important factor in successful group operation is skillful and sensitive membership behaviour. In an experienced and skilled group the members can work effectively with no leader at all. McGregor (1960) argues that creative commitment to organisational objectives requires unique kinds of interaction which can only occur in an effective group setting. Organisation development interventions are a way of achieving this and Quality Circle techniques are especially valuable for developing individuals as members of groups.

The work team is very important psychologically for most people, fulfilling needs for acceptance, satisfaction etc. People can identify with the successes of a small group in supporting its leader and solving problems. They want to increase their competence and satisfaction within the group. However most organisational cultures suppress feelings, an example of this would be the meeting in which few views are expressed but the members express their views to each other afterwards. This kind of atmosphere leads to reduced levels of trust, support and co-operation. Encouragement to express feelings, acceptance of feelings, and gathering data on feelings as a part of organisational culture leads to better goal setting, communications, conflict resolution etc.

Team building is a vital part of organisation development. Interventions frequently consist of diagnostic sessions away from the workplace in which the consultant interviews group members about how the group functions, what the problems are, and how it could function better. The consultant analyses and presents the interview data to the group which then begins work on solutions and establishes an action plan which may involve a Gestalt dimension, focussing on the individual and development of the whole person, encouraging the expression of their feelings and both their positive and negative characteristics in all their dealings. A role analysis technique might be used in which work roles are clarified by considering both the views of the focal role incumbent and the people he or she works with, gradually developing a role profile. Role negotiation can then take place with each party agreeing in writing to change certain behaviour in return for changes in the behaviour of others.

As mentioned earlier organisations are made up of overlapping work groups which help to determine culture. In part the style of management can be determined from the top since a subordinate in one group will be a leader in another and will tend to model himself on the leader of the first group. Culture may be characterised by trust, support and openness and teamwork, or by struggle, mistrust, and infighting. Organisation development will seek to work through teams to change processes, relationships and culture, over time, making lasting improvements in the organisation and once the results of this start to be seen in improved performance organisational subsystems such as appraisal, staffing, communications and compensation will need to change. Since improvements in interpersonal skills resulting from OD efforts will include the expression of feelings, feedback systems and their management need to be helpful. In particular a formal appeal system might be needed to protect individuals from anomalies in organisational culture, e.g. what if it became taboo to criticise the OD effort?

An organisation consists of inputs, an internal process, and outputs. It needs feedback processes to maintain efficiency and effectiveness and these need to be managed and linked. The whole structure could be ruined by paying too much attention to any one aspect while ignoring another. Subsystems include human/social, task, technological and changes can occur in any by influencing just one. In OD efforts the human/social subsystem tends to be tackled first. It is often seen as valuable to include key people from the output phase of the operation, such as representatives of client organisations, in the OD effort.

The OD consultant brings potentially new values to the organisation such as assumptions about interpersonal relationships. He or she knows about structuring activities so they are problem oriented with clear goals based on experiential learning and involving the whole person, including feelings, enabling people to learn about both task and process. The work team is always the main focus. The process always starts with diagnosis, then uses data collection and analysis, obtained through observation, questionnaires, observation of meetings etc. This is an action research model which aims to help the client organisation to generate valid data, to enable it to have free informed choice, and to help it generate internal commitment to the choices made. OD interventions are designed to improve the organisation's adapting, coping, and problem solving skills. Examples of techniques would include critique sessions at the end of meetings, and "mirroring" workshops to see how clients view the service. OD uses real problems, it is process based and aims to move the organisation towards greater effectiveness over time while acknowledging that perfection will never be achieved. The process is managed by constantly addressing issues of ownership, timing, relevance to organisational goals, effectiveness, and ramifications of a particular intervention on other aspects of the organisation, particularly its culture.

OD consultants are looking for improvements in interpersonal competence, a shift in values to raise the profile of human factors and feelings, improvements in team management, and better methods of resolving conflict. OD often needs to deal with tension, conflict, or competition between groups. In fact OD legitimises conflict as an area for collaborative management. Strategies include changing the members of groups and instituting a training programme, finding a goal that no group can achieve without help from others, and improving communications and interactions to emphasise intergroup co-operation as a means of achieving organisational goals. "Mirroring" in which the host group which is experiencing difficulties with other groups invites representatives from those groups to a meeting to provide feedback on their views of the host group. The consultant will often interview the people attending the meeting to get a sense of the problems and their magnitude. If the underlying problems relating to team malfunction need to be examined fishbowl techniques, sensitivity training laboratories, transactional analysis and life and career planning interventions can be introduced.

OD is about measuring against goals and targets but involving a much wider group to improve the utilisation of both human and technical resources. Action research is the key process, since it relates directly to a problem, e.g. unproductive weekly staff meetings. An action research approach to this problem might be to gather data in the form of views and opinions in the search for causes, generate hypotheses in terms of solutions, for example it might be appropriate to change the timings of meetings, the group might be more cohesive if it generated its own agenda, or if free discussion were allowed. Each hypothesis could then be tested, and evaluated. The solutions will have a much greater chance of "sticking" since the group will have generated them themselves and will therefore support them.

There are many factors that are vital in determining appropriate modes of OD intervention, such as the size of the organisation, top management must be aware of and must understand the problems in the organisation and must have a desire for improvement. For optimum success there must be use of an external consultant, and close involvement of team leaders. To promote the OD programme early successes via action research need to be achieved. OD successes should be linked to existing good practice in the organisation and the consultant should seek to build in to the OD effort the capacity to build on what he has introduced and an open educational philosophy towards OD. The organisation must not reward OD efforts on themselves, but must always look to performance.

The relationship between the consultant and the client is critical. The consultant should always make his or her philosophy and values clear, making it plain that he or she should not be considered an expert, but someone who is helping to solve problems. The consultant is committed to making work life more meaningful for all employees by providing more opportunities to contribute. He or she is interested in enhancing everyone's power, not in equalising power across the organisation. At first it is best if a single manager is the client, then as trust develops the whole organisation becomes the client since the consultant must work with those he or she is trying to influence. Interventions won't work if there is a suspicion that a policy is being imposed by top management via the consultant, or if the client has hidden motives such as wanting to promote the interests of subordinates. Amongst all the other issues that the OD intervention will examine are leadership style and ways of managing. The level of autocracy of top management is important, the consultant needs to consider whether top management really wants collaboration. The consultant must avoid being seen as "selling" a form of utopia when he or she is really helping clients with their problems. He or she can be an expert in the processes, but not in the task. The consultant must determine the depths of the intervention, just deep enough to produce enduring solutions while maintaining the continuing commitment of the client. The consultant must not be seduced into joining the culture of the organisation and must be honest about the point at which his or her commitment should cease. As change occurs the client must be encouraged to "let go" of the old systems and attitudes.

OD methods have a massive potential for success, drawing as they do on a wide range of models, theories and practices, including action research, a systems approach to understanding organisational dynamics and a change strategy which focuses on the culture of work teams and the organisation. However OD does have some drawbacks, it has been criticised on the basis that it is directed at the human and social dynamics of organisations rather than what could be considered to be the main task of business. Also the endless variations of OD make it very difficult to evaluate.

Quality Circles could be considered to be an OD programme, operating as they do using set techniques with work teams. OD methods will be recognised in the later description of the Quality Circle experiment at Accrington and Rossendale College. Quality Circles have a good record in industry and commerce where they appear to have improved employee motivation, assisted in problem solving, and contributed to better cost effectiveness. There are a number of examples of the use of Quality Circles in Educational Institutions in the United States including Universities, Community Colleges and local School Boards, but no examples of the use of Quality Circles in Educational Institutions in the U.K. with the exception of two Colleges which have both been involved in Quality Circles related activity but whose experiments bear a number of distinct differences from the standard Quality Circles format.

KEY QUALITY CIRCLE CONCEPTS

If a Quality Circle programme is going to work effectively a number of factors need to be taken into account by the management of an organisation.

The Need for Voluntary Participation

People are asked to join, often in a very discreet way. They participate in a process designed to allow them to influence management decisions about the work they do via the use of a number of techniques they have learned. Employees at all levels in the organisation are free to join, not to join, to drop out, or return.

The Need for Supportive Management

Perhaps the most critical factor. It doesn't matter how well the programme is designed or how enthusiastic the members are the programme will fail if management doesn't openly give support. Each Circle must know that management is appreciative and believes that everyone in the organisation has something to say and should be given the opportunity to say it.

A Belief in People Building and Development

McGregor's Theory Y assumes that people are basically hardworking, responsible and responsive to positive encouragement and trust. Quality Circle philosophy owes a great deal to this theory in that the whole concept is based on trust, caring, respect and a belief that people can and want to give more than they do. Over a period of time competence and co-operation is developed. It is wrong to implement a programme of Quality Circles with all its human relations potential simply to achieve short term cost benefits. People who have rarely, if ever, been asked to contribute must be given time to cope with this new opportunity.

The Probable Development of Leaders

Quality Circles almost always develop new leaders amongst the workforce, often people who have gone unnoticed over many years. The training given and the Quality Circle experience also tends to make existing leaders better ones through the morale and confidence generated.

The Need for Training

Adequate training in team building/working and Quality Circle techniques is an integral part of the programme. Members must come to grips with the power they have both to solve problems and effectively 'compel' assistance from the formal structure of the organisation. Training is important for Quality Circle Leaders and members because of their power to make or break a Circle programme it is also important for middle managers and senior managers.

MANAGEMENT OF A QUALITY CIRCLE PROGRAMME

The Management structure usually has seven elements although variations are possible. The Circle leader in the Industrial or Commercial context is usually the supervisor/foreman. He or she is the person most responsible for the success of the Circle. Circle members are usually drawn from a 'natural work group' and the size of Circle can vary from about 3-15 members although an ideal number is 7-10 members. The facilitator organises training, makes the necessary administrative arrangements and is responsible for the overall leadership and direction of the programme. The steering or co-ordinating committee includes the facilitator, Circle leaders, Senior Managers, Union Representatives, and gives coherence to the programme, group support to the Circle leaders, and ensures that the problems tackled are viable. Senior Managers must be seen to be giving appropriate support and resources if the programme is to succeed. Specialists, such as Computer Manager, Chief Caretaker, Chief Administrative Officer may be called in to advise during the problem solving process. The consultant is involved in training, working with the facilitator and steering committee, and advising Senior management. Programmes which haven't used a consultant have tended to fail.

QUALITY CIRCLE ACTIVITY

All Quality Circles meet ideally once a week and work to a strict code of conduct:

-Criticise ideas not people

-The only stupid question is the one not asked

-Everyone in the group is responsible for progress

-Be open to the ideas of others.

The techniques used are as follows:

Brainstorming

Occurs when each member of the Circle in turn contributes ideas which are progressively listed until no more ideas are forthcoming. The aim is to encourage uninhibited thinking to generate the largest number of ideas. Brainstorming is probably the most fundamental technique of the Quality Circle process and works because a group will always produce more than an individual, ideas will always give rise to other ideas, and as everyone is forced to participate on an equal basis, no-one can dominate. Brainstorming which is generally accompanied by some form of voting or ranking process can be used when a Quality Circle is looking for a problem, looking for the causes of a problem, looking for solutions to test more scientifically, or simply stuck.

Cause and Effect Classification

This is based on the fishbone diagram developed by Dr. Kaoru Ishikawa lecturer in Quality Control at Tokyo University. Once causes of a problem have been brainstormed they are allocated amongst the 4 headings on the diagram which are usually manpower, machines, methods and materials. (See Fig.1)

Figure 1

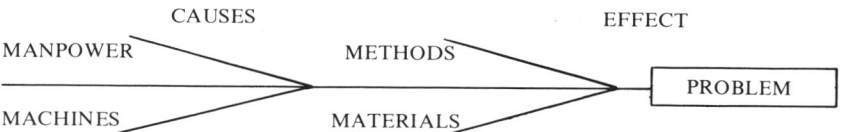

The headings can be varied depending on the problem. This process will start to give an indication of where most of the causes are originating from.

Data Collection

Often the Quality Circle will need more information to test whether the perceived causes of the problem are in reality the causes of the problem. Decisions need to be made such as what information is needed? Over what period? How should it be measured? Who will measure it? Some form of check sheet usually needs to be designed. In considering more intangible problems such as curriculum related problems a questionnaire approach may be best.

Pareto Analysis

Pareto was a 19th Century Italian economist who discovered the 80/20 rule in relation to national wealth, i.e. 80% of the wealth tends to be owned by 20% of the population. This ratio has since been shown to apply to many situations and is particularly useful in ranking the causes of problems in that 20% of the causes are often responsible for 80% of the problem. Pareto charts give a visual interpretation of the causes of problems which is often more helpful than a mass of figures and enables us to identify the vital few causes against the trivial many.

Figure 2

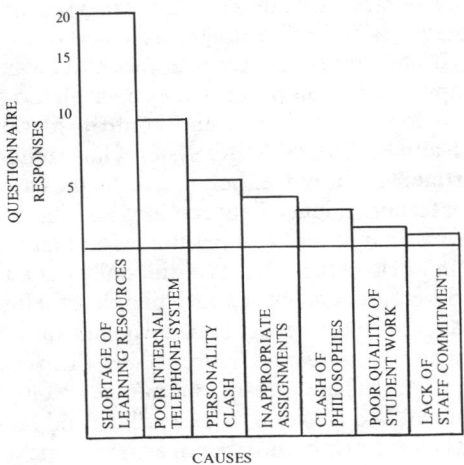

Example The problem being considered by a Quality Circle is 'Poor Relationship with the moderator' possible causes have been determined by brainstorming and cause and effect classification, confirmation is sought by a questionnaire to all relevant staff and then illustrated by a Pareto chart. (See Fig.2)

Presentation to Management

Quality Circles tend to shy away from presentations and often they aren't strictly necessary since a Circle can independently implement many of the solutions reached. However, presentations are important since they are the conclusion of the problem solving process. They are a means of impressing management, enhancing the Quality Circle's reputation, ensuring the acceptance of solutions and gaining publicity for the work of the Circle. They aid communication within the organisation since presentations can be reported on and they give great satisfaction to those involved, developing their skills in the process. Quite often a Circle which appears to be reaching the burn out stage is rejuvenated by a successful presentation.

Quality Circle techniques appear simple. However, in operation they become rather more complex often needing to be refined and adapted in various ways to cope with varying problems.

QUALITY CIRCLES IN THE U.K.

Current Interest

The problem with new management concepts in the U.K. is that they tend to be abandoned when they prove more difficult to implement than was originally thought, management by objectives in the 1960s was an example of this. Management by objectives relates to systems of joint target setting and performance review between supervisors and subordinates designed to increase the focus on organisation goals. It has proved a successful technique when associated with collaborative team approaches but programmes have all too often been used in an autocratic way to force compliance and confirm hierarchical structures. According to French and Bell (1978) MBO Systems have tended to be promoted by personnel departments without either much diagnosis of the problem or acknowledging the interdependence between jobs and has often led to defensiveness, impaired performance and competition within teams when associated with implied criticism. British firms have traditionally put a massive amount of time into technical developments but not into people development. In spite of this Quality Circles appear to have caught on and gone from strength to strength over the last 7 years with more and more major firms becoming involved including a number of famous and prestigious names amongst firms both large and small such as Jaguar, Wedgewood, ICL, Mullard and Honeywell. This has caused a great deal of interest with a number of articles appearing in the national press all of which have been fulsome in their praise of the concept. For example, David Felton writing in The Independent (19/1/87) points out that ICL has had no serious industrial disputes since it started Quality Circles 4 years ago and quotes the ICL Quality Programme and Communications Manager as saying

"We are a single status company and Quality Circles have helped enormously to break down the traditional barriers inside the plant".

Ronald Faux writing in the Times (20/1/87) argues strongly for the involvement of workers in the management of companies via Quality Circles if policies are to be followed through and performance improved. The public sector is not neglected in this press interest and the Chief Executive of Windsor and Maidenhead, an authority much praised by the audit commission for its management initiatives writing in the Times (Blacker 12/3/87) explains the difficulties of getting people to perform well in comfortable and protected situations. His answer is very similar to a Quality Circle approach based on team building amongst natural work groups which then identify problems, analyse tasks and set their own targets using customer service as the critical thread in determining performance.

Success and Failure in Quality Circle Programmes

Bartlett (1983) in a study for the M.S.C. found that American owned companies proved more successful in supporting Quality Circle programmes. Those firms looking for immediate benefits from Circles tended to be disappointed since the benefits in terms of commitment and motivation amongst the workforce came over a much longer period. He also found that when more time was devoted to preparation prior to starting Circles, the greater was the likelihood of success. In particular the use of an outside consultant to present the concept to the workforce was vital. Management attitudes are critical but problems have not come from senior managers who have found it relatively easy to be committed, they have come from middle managers who may well feel threatened by Circles, possibly led by their subordinates, whose activities are not made clear until the reporting stage. Union attitudes have sometimes been blamed for the failure of Quality Circle programmes. This is not the case, the T.U.C. in its policy statement in July, 1981, while implicitly critical of the technique because of the potential threat to the collective bargaining role of unions, has not discouraged the spread of Circles. Where Circles have failed the fault lies with management, not unions. In the Bartlett survey (1983) failed programmes were characterised by:-

-Inadequate support given by management

-Ignoring the voluntary principle in the recruiting of leaders, members and in attempting to programme the activities of the circles

-Failure to commit resources to training, communication, and the use of an outside consultant

-Failure to commit enough time to the facilitator.

Dale and Lees (1986) have also considered what constitutes failure in Quality Circles. The obvious answer is when the Circle stops meeting but in practice achievements elsewhere in the Quality Circle programme can lead to a moribund Circle meeting again so as not to be outdone. It could be that some circles have a limited life anyway coming into existence to solve a particular range of problems and disbanding when this work is done. Some firms may attempt to measure the costs of running Quality Circles and deem the programme a failure if these costs aren't outweighed by the savings made. This approach however does not take into account the massive peripheral benefits of Quality Circles since even when a Circle ceases to operate the techniques learned and behavioural and attitudinal changes in former members can still be beneficial. Quality Circles too can be seen as an interim device in moving towards a more participative management system and culture, and in these circumstances when a Circle programme ends it cannot be deemed a failure if it leads on to another phase in the change process.

Integration of Circle Programmes

Quality Circles potentially have tremendous power, and there are many instances where solutions to problems have been rejected by workers when suggested by managers, but accepted when suggested by Circles. At present, however, Circles tend to be appendages to other systems and aren't accountable. Some even feel that any attempt at evaluation is contrary to the spirit of Circles. If Circles are to be fully absorbed into the fabric of organisations, relationships will have to be established. One way to integrate them would be to make Quality Circles part of a Department's normal activities using middle managers as facilitators. In this way managers cease to be threatened by circle development and can share in the success of the programme. Another way of integrating circles into the management of organisations might be through the development of management circles which are at present very rare. Dale and Lees (1986) argue that management should take a pro-active approach by providing written guidelines for managers in maintaining and supporting circles and also training circles in self analysis to prevent them from blaming others, particularly management, for their own failings. Most Circles up to the present have involved blue collar workers and it could well be that the full potential of circles will not be achieved until multi-disciplinary circles and management circles are developed.

Criticism of Quality Circles

Not all writers on Quality Circles implicitly accept that Quality Circles are appropriate to western organisations. Dore (1983) argues that the Quality Circle concept demands trust that both workers and management will benefit from improved productivity in an equal way, and that once the trust is there workers may well find that looking for ways of doing the job better through Quality Circles can make their lives more interesting. In Japan, where Quality Circles have flourished the trust is there, workers have job security and wages are based on seniority and wage scales which look for fairness throughout working life. Dore considers that consultants who sell Quality Circles as a bolt on feature to a firm are fraudulent and that for Quality Circles to work in Britain managements must accept a greater commitment to their workforce, particularly in traditional industries. In Japan workers belong to their company, in Britain workers work for their company. In Japan managers are more involved, expecting to work as hard as the workforce who believe the managers are employed on merit. In Britain managers are more aloof and there are still class distinctions. Quality Circles may blur the lines between 'us and them' but for real success they require a more open and trusting approach throughout an organisation. Dore believes that since U.K. organisations are only using Quality Circles in an attempt to emulate Japanese economic success they will, in fact, only serve the traditional aims of increased profits and squeezing more from the workers and will inevitably fail, since we cannot emulate Japanese social and cultural values.

Bradley and Hill (1983) are also sceptical of the effectiveness of Quality Circle programmes in Western organisations pointing out the difficulties of transferring the technique from Japan with its strong tradition of high trust between management and workforce, consensus in meeting organisational objectives and emphasis on group work and collective responsibility, to the Western context characterised by emphasis on individual effort and reward, low trust between management and workers and no consensus over organisational objectives between shareholders and management on one side and the workforce on the other. Traditional western styles of industrial relations have been adversarial. Quality and efficiency have been seen mainly as tasks for management specialists rather than rank and file employees.

In analysing these hypotheses together with other social aspects of Quality Circles based on research in British and American companies with Quality Circle programmes, Bradley and Hill (1983) discovered that most workers did, in fact, believe that they had more to offer their organisations and Quality Circles were a way of doing this. Also Quality Circles made more information available which increased awareness of managerial problems and improved communications generally. However, it was felt that management continued to withhold information and criticism of this increased the longer that a circle was in existence. Trades Unions were thought to have benefited to some extent from the increased information which had been made available to Quality Circles and although Quality Circles can be a device for organisations to communicate direct with workers, by-passing union structures they have not, in fact, greatly changed workers' distrust of management or reduced support for workplace unionism. Quality Circle programmes had caused some dissension between Quality Circle members and non-members who had to cover for them during meetings or modify their work behaviour to accommodate circle suggestions. There was some feeling that those who joined circles tended to be pro-management anyway. Middle managers saw Quality Circles both as a threat and an implied criticism feeling that if they had been seen to be doing a good job the circle programme wouldn't have been necessary and while they were unlikely to openly oppose circles they did attempt to influence them subtly to keep control by, for example, persuading circle leaders to promote issues in the circle which the manager saw as acceptable. It was felt that with these pressures operating there would be problems in sustaining circle programmes in the long term.

Similarities between the Private Sector and Education

When considering the problems involved in setting up Quality Circles in Education it is important to remember that some industrial and commercial activities have problems too. In particular there are many parallels between the service sector and educational organisations. The problems tackled tend to be intangible and it is, therefore, difficult to evaluate benefits. There are problems of finding a common meeting time leading to poor attendance and some departments or sections consist of small numbers of employees which points towards the formation of multi-disciplinary circles. There is often difficulty in selecting problems which are relevant to all members, with solutions often involving changes to systems and procedures which rely on others elsewhere in the organisation, who may not be sympathetic to circles. If the organisation is large, system changes may be proposed elsewhere which negate solutions proposed by circles.

Dale and Lees (1986) who have investigated the development of Quality Circle programmes in a diverse range of organisations, including the service sector, suggest that in the above circumstances there are a number of issues which should be addressed by managements, all of which are relevant to managements in the educational context. The management style may be too autocratic and the organisational structure too rigid (Dale and Lees 1986 P.9) for circles to succeed particularly if there is no history of employee participation, or the preparation may have been inadequate leading to a widespread lack of approval and lack of knowledge. This would be particularly critical if middle managers were sceptical. The circle programme may simply not have been given enough time to develop before being written off as a failure and the facilitator may be discouraged because of the difficulties of evaluating the benefits of circles dealing with intangible problems. Finally, both circles and the organisation generally need to be clear about their first priority, client service.

Quality Circles, however, in both the service sector generally and in education particularly, have far more potential than in capital intensive manufacturing organisations because they are labour intensive and have massive scope for people development.

Quality Circle Experiments in Educational Organisations in the U.K.

In view of the development of Quality Circle programmes in commerce, industry and the public sector in the U.K. and in the educational sector in the U.S. there is clearly scope for them to be tried in educational settings in the U.K. The experience elsewhere indicates that they could prove a useful tool for developing criteria for an educational audit within institutions. They could also be of great value in staff development terms especially for support staff who have long been neglected in Colleges even though they have a clear role in curriculum development. There have already been two experiments related to Quality Circles in Colleges in Britain, at High Peak College, conducted by M.J. Field and A.B. Harrison and at Barnfield College Luton, conducted by C. Blundell. However, both bear distinct differences from the pure Quality Circles concept. At High Peak College, individual Quality Circles were allowed to agree their own rules and methods of operating, not necessarily in common with other Quality Circles. For example some circles concerned themselves solely with curriculum issues, administrative problems were not allowed. Because of the value of the professional time taken up by circles another circle decided that each meeting must produce an activity, lesson or set of learning materials.

Two examples are given of Quality Circle operation. The first circle was for social and life skills staff which met in the members' own time, usually evenings. The problem was normally presented by the leader in general terms and questions were then invited. The group then broke up- into smaller groups to discuss the problem and identify likely solutions using a flip chart. The full group then re-assembled to fully discuss all suggested solutions as presented on the flip chart sheets. The small groups then decided on their ideal solutions which were debated again by the full group and once a solution was agreed on it was written up and distributed to all staff associated with social and life skills. Problems handled in this way included planning and evaluation, literacy problems, and the place of counselling.

The second example involved general studies staff. The circle met in work time and each member brought an item of work they wanted to discuss or try out on other circle members. Then through open discussion the work was evaluated and amended if necessary before being adopted by other circle members. Examples of topics included use of simulation games in communications, the design of BTEC assignments, and role playing.

As part of this quality circle activity time limits were imposed to ensure progress and the limits of Quality Circle authority were clearly defined. Problems or issues to be considered were not always decided on by the circles themselves but were sometimes allocated by management and the work of the circles did not always involve the solution of problems since at times the circles discussed aspects of work or shared learning materials. This way of operating should be compared with the pure Quality Circle concepts of voluntarism, rigorous training, autonomy in deciding what problems to tackle, and the strict use of the techniques of brainstorming, cause and effect classification, pareto analysis, data collection, and management presentation, whilst adhering to the Quality Circle code of conduct.

-Criticise ideas not people

-The only stupid question is the one not asked

-Be open to the ideas of others

-Everyone in the group is responsible for progress.

The Quality Circle programme at Barnfield College Luton was begun by the professional tutor who saw them as a vehicle for his staff development activities with both "management and shop floor". The usual starting point was the circulation of a paper to departmental staff describing Quality Circles, how they operated in commerce and industry and their relevance to the educational context. This was followed by explanatory meetings with participating groups of staff. There were great demands on the professional tutors "facilitator" role as the circles got going, but this initial dependence proved helpful since it gradually gave groups the confidence to do things for themselves, valuable "unobtrusive" training in how to take responsibility. Gradually co-ordinators or circle leaders emerged.

Quality Circles at Barnfield College Luton were defined simply as groups coming together to share ideas on any education related problem. However importance was placed on clearly defining the problem and working to a code of conduct. Membership was mixed with management involved but in an equal, non-vetoing sense. The circles initially proved undisciplined in dealing with the techniques, mainly related to brainstorming but this gradually changed as they became more tolerant and open.

From the start Quality Circle meetings were distinguished from other meetings. Attendance was voluntary, although during work time (exceptionally it was made compulsory amongst one group of staff). Meetings were to last for one hour, subject matter was to be agreed in advance, so that members could prepare, the leadership would rotate, and comprehensive notes would be made of each meeting to provide feedback. It was decided that students could benefit from involvement in Quality Circles and learning the techniques, since many will work for firms which have well established circle programmes.

Early in the programme it became apparent that educational problems can be far more complex than industrial problems being more conceptual. Consequently some of the issues considered have not related strictly to problem solving in the Quality Circles sense, one circle met simply to exchange views on educational philosophy, but other circles have taken a more direct approach, one considering teaching performance in the classroom which led to demands for micro-teaching exercises. Other problems considered have included counselling, problem students, stress and frustration, time management, communications, mentoring new tutors, interviewing, and teaching methods.

It was discovered that once a Quality Circle was an accepted and valued feature of faculty life attendance became routine and participation lively. In one school there was an interesting link between the informal structure represented by Quality Circles and the formal structure in that the circles were used to generate material for official staff meetings which in turn determined problems for circles to consider.

At Barnfield College Luton Blundell (1986) identified the traditional benefits normally claimed for Quality Circles such as a greater sense of corporate identity and pride, improved awareness of corporate goals, improved decision making and problem solving skills, improved communication and self confidence, development of leadership skills, and better relationships between workers and management. He also recognised that circles could be a threat to an uncertain management. Field and Harrison (1983) identified some powerful benefits relating to their experience of Quality Circles at High Peak College such as:

-Group support in the face of imposed change from BTEC, MSC, etc.

-Changed ways of working through team building

-The breaking down of an ethos which has emphasised individual achievement since Quality Circles have proved able to satisfy both the desire for individual achievement and the group process with its implied safety and belonging

-An understanding of the need for curriculum decisions to be taken by those who are going to implement them

-The promotion of the concept of 'ownership' of policy and growth of awareness of corporate objectives.

There are indications in the above experiments that the rather more freewheeling approaches used at both High Peak College and Barnfield College Luton may be more appropriate to the consideration of complex educational and curriculum issues than the more rigid standard Quality Circle model adopted from commerce and industry and used in the Accrington and Rossendale College experiment.

THE NORTH AMERICAN EXPERIENCE OF QUALITY CIRCLES IN EDUCATIONAL INSTITUTIONS

Quality Circles have been tried in all sectors of American education over the last seven years, principally in the University sector, but also in community colleges, and local school administration. One of the main reasons for trying Quality Circles has been a growing public dissatisfaction with the educational system at a time of severe financial constraints. Bandy (1984) points to the one attribute education and industry share, public distrust of their products. American cars and high school graduates are perceived as not being as good as they used to be! Quality Circles have been seen as a way of enhancing morale and improving the service, and while all writers stress that they aren't a panacea they have nonetheless been seen as a way of dealing with all problems from the difficulties caused by a segmented curriculum to discipline on the school bus.

Bandy (1984) in writing about the Quality Circle programme at the Illinois State Board of Education points out that since 70% of education budgets are allocated to salaries staff are the greatest resource which needs to be maximised by treating them as adults, and partners, with dignity and respect. Quality Circles were seen as one way of doing this by improving morale and making procedures more efficient. At its height the programme had 15 circles representing all but two departments, taking an average 4 months to complete a project with over 90% of recommendations accepted. Problems dealt with have included 5 on the physical environment, four on communication and two on information retrieval. Evaluation has been on the basis of questionnaires following presentations including questions to managers such as "How well defined was the problem?" "How well did the solution fit the problem?" and "How well did the data support the presentation?" Questions to circle members included "Describe your perception about how management understood and received your presentation". Respondents replied with very positive comments such as "The circle provides a safe environment for expressing differing or negative points of view".

Galbraith and Christian (1986) argue that in view of the potential benefits of circles and the constant demands for 'excellence in education', it would have been logical for educational institutions to be leaders in Quality Circle development, but they are not because of:

    -The almost total absence of participatory management styles

    -The operation of hundreds of committees

    -The lack of an overall authority responsible for Quality Control

– The concept of 'academic freedom' which can be a synonym for competing interests and inability to define the product.

Skibbens (1986) recognises the benefits of Circles in that the problems to be solved are selected by those experiencing difficulties, not an authority figure, therefore there is a far greater chance of a lasting solution. The process of solving the problem gives feelings of great satisfaction to participants, it makes them realise their worth to the organisation. The process means that the solutions are owned by many people, they are recommended for acceptance and widely discussed, not implemented unilaterally. However there are many blocks to implementing Quality Circle programmes since some administrators and school boards have trouble even admitting that problems exist let alone that subordinates and lay people can create better solutions than they can. In fact Quality Circles have been around long enough for them not to be considered new but an established technique of improving morale by involving a committed and resourceful staff in solving problems.

It seems that the lack of a participatory management style or support from top management has inhibited Quality Circle programmes in North American Education. The programmes which have succeeded best in the short term have been those which have had the most energy devoted to them by those fairly low in the hierarchy, initially anticipating increasing management support. When this failed to materialise failure of the programmes was inevitable.

An object lesson on how not to set up a Quality Circle programme is provided by Lawson and Tubbs (1986) writing of their experience with a research project at the University of Central Florida. Three pilot circles were set up in student support service areas. All met difficulties such as poor middle management support, poor initial problem selection, improper structuring of circle activities, participation not entirely voluntary, failure to adequately publicise circle activities and achievements, feelings of manipulation and scepticism leading to problems of finding appropriate meeting times.

The Health Center Circle made a number of minor improvements to procedures such as setting aside a separate room for immunisations during registration week, but almost all problems considered touched upon professional medical matters. This led to tension and the Quality Circle was disbanded. The student Center Circle failed and disbanded when its initial problem, "There is a need for a better understanding of the role and scope of the departments of Student Center and Student Government", proved far too complex. The Housing Circle failed when meetings became irregular after staff proved unable to adhere to Quality Circle processes, jumping between problems.

This short and somewhat unpleasant experience led the authors to conclude that Quality Circles are not compatible with all work environments and the industrial/commercial model is not relevant to education when management is not participative and staff are not used to group decision making by consensus even though a campus may have hundreds of committees. However, closer reading of the evidence indicates the need for a much more thorough going evaluation and assessment of the work situation prior to establishing the Quality Circle programme, the need for adequate resourcing and management support, much better communication, and information giving, and a much stronger emphasis on the voluntary principle. It did not help in this instance that the authors were attempting to lead a Quality Circle programme from the position of research students.

Some benefits of Quality Circles can be measured easily. In business settings there are often savings of money following Circle activity. This is also possible in education, for example a Quality Circle in the College of Business and Public Administration at the University of Missouri - Colombia considered the problem of poor commercial learning materials. As an alternative the Circle developed handouts, case studies, simulations, and other training materials and as a result of its recommendations students were saved some $18000-$20000. The effects of Quality Circle activity on participants is more difficult to quantify but attempts have been made in American Colleges to 'prove' the effectiveness of Quality Circles scientifically and one such was carried out at Iowa State University by Carol Kay and Kim Buch, using questionnaires, rating scales, and performance appraisals of circle members in three key areas of absenteeism, work quality and productivity, compared with a control group of non circle members. Such 'hard criteria' are commonly used in assessing the impact of organisational interventions. Attempts were also made to measure attitude changes before and during circle activity. The results seemed to indicate that circle members experienced an increase in job satisfaction, although this declined over time and were made more aware of the organisational climate, teamwork and communications. They also produced a higher quality of work and were more productive, in the year following circle implementation, achieving significant personal growth in the process. They were, however, less tolerant of colleagues who were not Quality Circle members and Quality Circle membership made little difference to absenteeism (although the Quality Circle group included two pregnancies and one person undergoing major surgery).

As part of the information gathering exercise associated with this monograph a questionnaire was sent to a number of American Colleges who were running Quality Circle programmes. Seven Colleges replied comprising five Universities in the United States, one Canadian University, one Canadian Community College, and one Community College in the United States. They were the

University of Cincinnati, the University of Montana, the University of Texas, Lane Community College, the University of Western Ontario, Southern Illinois University, Iowa State University and Cambrian College Ontario. All of these Colleges had very small Quality Circle programmes relative to the size of the organisations (25,000 students and 7,000 staff was not unusual in the larger Universities). The largest Quality Circle programmes were at Iowa State University (8 circles) and the University of Texas at Austin (7 circles). All the programmes were recent in origin, the oldest being one at Lane Community College which started in 1981 but was not currently in operation. The only programme listing circles of teaching staff was at Iowa State University, all other programmes consisting of support staff in library, administration, and technician areas of work, although academic staff were involved at facilitator level. A number of the programmes didn't in fact have a single facilitator but operated with a cadre of facilitators.

Problems dealt with by Circles have included administrative and related problems, work flow, communications, safety, office arrangements and traffic, accounting, operational/procedural problems, the development of a new faculty counselling system, inefficient telephone systems, adequate office time coverage, supply inventory control, and problems relating to the physical environment.

Among benefits of Quality Circles listed are improved employee work performance, increased job satisfaction, increased participation in decision making, improved team work and cohesiveness, 'ownership' of solutions which improves implementation, improved morale and confidence, cost savings, greater efficiency and involvement of all levels of staff. All of these are typical of benefits found elsewhere through Quality Circle programmes.

Many problems in the operation of circle programmes are also listed including lack of administrative support, shortage of funds, employee apathy, time constraints, difficulties of co-ordinating meeting times, inadequate time allocated for facilitating the programme, slowness of management in responding to solutions, shortage of management support generally, some circles suffering from burn out and lack of interest. At one College the biggest single problem was of circle leadership in that a 'supervisor' was often a circle leader but this was a source of conflict since the circle is a democratic activity and Supervisors often couldn't cope with a 'two hatted role'. Also members were fearful of repercussions afterwards if they stated controversial views in circle meetings. The solution in this case turned out to be shared leadership which provided for leader development, work sharing and a more supportive group environment.

In three instances the problems in running circles had led to programmes ceasing altogether. However, in one case verteams were now operating. Verteams are ad hoc problem solving groups which use Quality Circle techniques and processes but disband after proposing solutions to the identified problem. In other instances too Quality Circle techniques were being used outside the Quality Circle context.

Figures from the Quality Circle Network in Education, operated from Oklahoma State University confirm that while Quality Circle programmes in industry in North America are increasing in number they are declining in Educational Institutions from a high point in the early 1980s. Two examples of this are particularly disappointing given the obvious energy, enthusiasm and optimism which went into them at the start. These are Piedmont Community College, which from a high point of 17 Circles now has none, and Illinois School Board whose 15 circles have disappeared albeit with some major successes in terms of projects completed. Other programmes too are moribund. What is clear from a number of articles (Schafer 1983, Lane 1983, Bandy 1984, Lawson and Tubbs 1986, Skibbens 1986) is that even though programmes had massive support from those at a fairly low level in the hierarchy, who argued strongly for Quality Circles to become an integral component of management processes, they in fact failed to become of central importance to Institutions and died as a result.

Schafer (1983) writing of the Quality Circle experience at Lane Community College expands on this, pointing out that to succeed a Quality Circle programme needs significant changes in an organisation's managerial style and if Managers don't become interested in participation via an interpersonal style of management, they will rapidly go the way of other fads demoralising staff as they fade away. Quality Circles potentially reduce the need for middle Managers who, therefore, become concerned with job security, salaries and future opportunities in the organisation.

Perhaps the way forward for Quality Circles in American education is indicated by Lane (1983). In explaining William Ouchi's Theory Z, a development from McGregor's Theory Y in which Ouchi argues for the merging of Japanese managerial principles such as group planning and consensus decision making with the American work environment which encourages individualism. Theory Z places special emphasis on commitment to an explicit philosophy of action, long term commitment to employees, trust and high levels of participation. Lane (1983) argues that a Theory Z approach could solve two perennial problems of American education, inadequate supportive relationships for teachers, and the need to develop a holistic rather than a segmented curriculum. What is certain is that unless managerial attitudes are fundamentally changed Quality Circles have a very limited future in North American Educational Systems.

Chapter 2

THE INTRODUCTION OF A QUALITY CIRCLES PROGRAMME AT ACCRINGTON AND ROSSENDALE COLLEGE

BACKGROUND

Accrington and Rossendale College is a medium sized institution with 200 full time teaching staff and 100 support staff offering a wide range of non advanced further education courses to the 150,000 people in its catchment area on 8 major college sites. Like similar F.E. establishments it is faced with radical and rapid changes in the F.E. environment. Colleges are accused of inadequate awareness of industrial needs and of being out of date. They are said to be sluggish in response, outmoded in administrative arrangements, rigid in delivery styles, inattentive to workplace based experience, inefficient and costly. Competition has been encouraged with the mushrooming of private training agencies, many partly paid for with public money. A number of influential companies and managing agencies for YTS are turning from colleges to exclusively in-house training, some with computer assisted learning, work based assignment learning packs, and mobile tutors. Because of these trends the salaries and conditions of service of F.E. staff are under threat.

The number of traditional day release craft and vocational students has dramatically declined in recent years and there is now a decline in the recruitment of other 16-19 year olds as their numbers as a proportion of total population fall.

Whole vocational areas such as engineering and construction have declined to be replaced with a growing service sector such as tourism, catering and hairdressing. Learning styles are changing, there is a growing emphasis on open learning, resource based learning, and competence based learning all of which challenge traditional classroom teaching. Examination boards are developing new courses based on integrated curriculum, transferable skills and vocational sampling which demand new forms of cross College organisation and teaching competencies which prevent teachers from operating independently.

Increasingly funding for courses and equipment is coming from non LEA sources such as the European Social Fund, Manpower Services Commission and from the private sector paying full economic rates for courses. Colleges are expected to meet the needs of the whole community which involves hosting many education related activities such as jobclubs, playschemes, and community programmes, and to provide access routes to education for disadvantaged groups. Most Colleges are now open for at least 48 weeks each year. Financial controls are becoming tighter as LEAs introduce computer systems for controlling budgets. In some cases relationships between Colleges and LEAs are becoming strained as they fail to realise the breadth of work that Colleges are involved in and as Colleges become increasingly independent of them, e.g. setting up College Companies to handle income generating activities.

Because of restricted recruitment and promotion prospects the staffs in many colleges have a high average age profile. Many members of staff have difficulties in understanding and coming to terms with the changes outlined above. Bernstein (1971) has touched upon this problem pointing out that while senior staff have traditionally had horizontal work relationships with their peers in other subject hierarchies, junior staff have had only vertical work relationships within their own department or subject discipline, their horizontal relationships having been based on non task based contacts. Since promotions have tended to come through subject expansion, inter departmental rivalry has always been there. The demands of an integrated curriculum are for changed relationships based on co-operation. Staff from a number of subject disciplines must now work together in planning, delivering, reviewing and evaluating their courses in response to demands from many sides which inevitably leads to stress. Management structures in Colleges have failed to reflect the extent of change. They have remained relatively rigid and hierarchical, unused to cross departmental cooperation, and are suffering from strains in attempting to accommodate the new curriculum.

Accrington and Rossendale College has to a greater or lesser extent experienced all of these difficulties and uncertainties and as a result our staff has suffered problems of morale, motivation, a lack of clarity of career aims and difficulties in identifying with College objectives. This has not been helped by a general lack of sympathy with existing methods of consultation and participation in decision making.

Quality Circles operate alongside but separate from existing management structures and in the light of a strong commitment from senior management seemed to offer the College a means of introducing an adaptable method of participatory management which could well prove effective. While it was evident that there would always be some resistance from middle managers at Senior Lecturer and Section Leader level who might see Quality Circles as a threat to their authority and from some class teachers who in the face of any change tend to fall back on their traditional classroom role and relationship with 'my students' it seemed to be well worth the attempt.

PLANNING AND PREPARATION FOR A QUALITY CIRCLE PROGRAMME

Experience in commercial and industrial organisations has shown that effective implementation of Quality Circle programmes has only taken place when outside consultants have been involved who have been able to analyse and take an objective view of existing management structures to determine the likely success of Quality Circles. Hence at an early stage of the planning process an approach was made to Maurice Alston of Employee Development and Motivation Consultants, a firm with a proven track record of introducing Quality Circles into firms both large and small, and public agencies, notably hospitals. Agreement on a consultancy fee was quickly reached with EDMC and protracted negotiations began with FEU over project funding during the Spring, Summer and Autumn of 1985. Eventually a start date of 1st January 1986 became possible.

The aims of the project agreed with FEU were as follows:

-to involve staff in participatory management

-to evolve and test a Quality Circle model which is transferable to other institutions

-to evaluate the effectiveness of the model

-to evaluate Quality Circles as a process of Staff Development.

A Literature Search was undertaken at this stage to inform our Quality Circles experiment as it developed. Current thinking about Quality Circles and the experience of other U.K. organisations and American Educational organisations using Quality Circles is reviewed elsewhere in this report. A detailed bibliography is attached to the monograph. It was important at an early stage for the consultants to gain an impression of the likely success of Quality Circles in the College and this was done in three ways:

-A meeting of a group of 'Opinion Formers' was held on 6th January, 1986. The group which included the Principal, Vice Principals, Heads of Department and key administrative and support staff had the concept explained to them by the consultant and were able to ask questions. Several days later they were interviewed individually and asked a number of pre-determined questions to elicit their expectations of the project. Their responses listed as benefits (see page 45) became important in the planning of the presentation of the concept to all staff in the College.

-On 3rd February, 1986 I, as project director and facilitator, underwent a one day training course at the office of EDMC at Bradford. This included close questioning about the organisational and administrative structure of the college, as a democratic style of operation is necessary if a Quality Circle Programme is to flourish (See Fig.3).

-Since the support of the Principal would be crucial to the implementation of any solutions to problems that Quality Circles might suggest it was important to get an early commitment from him, and this commitment was made clear both in early meetings with staff and in statements made and minuted at the first meeting of the project steering committee on February 4th 1986.

The next important stage in the process of preparation came when all staff were invited to meetings on the three major sites of the College. At these meetings staff were informed of the purpose of Quality Circles together with their background and the way they operated in practice. Staff were given the opportunity to comment, ask questions, and give their views about the relevance of Quality Circles to the College. Staff comment was muted although there was some hostility to the idea amongst some staff who saw Quality Circles as yet another non-classroom activity which took them away from their students. The principle of voluntarism and the availability of paid cover to enable Circles to meet were stressed. Some staff were worried about training for Circle leadership if this resulted in leading a Circle which might include a 'sullen' section leader who feared that his or her authority was being usurped. In general, although there was some interested discussion and questioning, the reaction was an apathetic one.

As a follow up to these meetings the Consultant was invited to visit the College on the 10th February, 1986 to talk to members of staff at random to ascertain their reactions to the mass meetings and to gauge the likelihood of staff volunteering for Circle Leader Training. At this stage he was fairly pessimistic about the possibilities of success. There seemed to be some suspicion of the Principal's motives in introducing the concept of Quality Circles and what was seen as the Principal's rather autocratic style of management also seemed to be a potential disincentive. It was decided that it would be helpful for the Principal to issue a statement to all staff indicating his views on Quality Circles and emphasising the principle of voluntarism, in particular the fact that no-one would in any way be criticised for not volunteering. At the same time the Principal detailed his own expectations of the Quality Circles project:

-That it would demonstrate that he wasn't only interested in a hierarchical system of management even though this was structural in further education and could be useful at times.

-That it would demonstrate his belief that the quality of what people say was not connected with their status in the College, and that everyone had a right to be heard.

-That it would show that the College would benefit from a more participative approach to ensure cohesion because of the way it had grown over recent years.

-That the skills and techniques of information gathering and decision making developed through Quality Circles could be used to good effect in other areas of College work.

As part of the debate about the Quality Circles project a special meeting of the Academic Board was held to determine what kind of role the Academic Board should take regarding the monitoring of the project. The views of the Academic Board reflected the ambivalence felt by staff. The Academic Board while approving and supporting the project wanted to play no direct role in it, preferring to leave it entirely to the Facilitator. There was heated debate at this stage amongst Heads of Department about just how staff should be approached and asked about volunteering for Circle Leader Training without apparently being coerced, since it was decided that any approach by a member of 'management' such as a Head of Department or Section Leader might be deemed to be to a certain extent intimidatory thereby destroying the concept of voluntarism. It was decided that 'neutral' intermediaries would be used who would simply collect names and forward them to the Facilitator. It was quite surprising in view of the earlier apathy when 19 people volunteered for Circle Leader Training and it proved necessary to hold two courses during March and April 1986.

QUALITY CIRCLE LEADER TRAINING

Leader Training was conducted via two three day courses held at the most suitable College Centre by the Consultant. It consisted of an introduction to the Quality Circles concept, detailed explanation, discussion and practice of the key concepts of brainstorming, data collection, Pareto Analysis, cause and effect classification, presentation of findings along with leadership and group exercises. The course also included discussion of the operation of a Quality Circle programme via the work of a co-ordinating committee and facilitator. The first course consisted of seven members of the teaching staff, one member of the library staff and two members of the administrative staff. The course proved a very pleasant three day experience, there being no obvious divisions between the three categories of staff involved, and so the course could be regarded as a useful staff development exercise in itself. The problem of what constituted a natural work group was never satisfactorily solved, i.e. whether it was a subject group, or staff workroom group, or section group, or Departmental group. Also the examples of problems chosen to illustrate the working of Quality Circle techniques were unsatisfactory in that they were insoluble, e.g. the problem of minibuses, the problem of a multi-site College. However, this demonstrated that problems needed to be broken down, and that Quality Circles were not going to immediately solve problems which had existed for many years. Perhaps the course was too pleasant an experience since whilst participants were convinced of the usefulness of Quality Circle techniques, by the end of the course they lacked the missionary zeal necessary to go out and form circles. This applied particularly to members of the teaching staff.

The second Quality Circle Leader Training Course consisted of seven members of the teaching staff, one member of the library staff and one member of the technician staff. It followed the same pattern as the first course and again proved a very pleasant learning experience for the participants. Since none of the participants on the first course, a month earlier, had succeeded in forming circles, the final afternoon of the second course consisted of all 19 trained circle leaders, together with the Consultant and Facilitator considering the best way forward. One member of the administrative staff and one member of the teaching staff were confident of forming their own circle. Two members of the library staff, working together, felt they could form a circle. It was decided that the remaining trained Circle Leaders would form two circles and that if the leaders intent on forming their own circles were unsuccessful over a two week period they too would join these trained leaders' groups. At this stage, therefore, there were potentially five Quality Circles. The problem of the natural work group was never really solved and in the end was ignored. Although seen as generally important in the successful operation of a Quality Circle programme perhaps its importance in the educational context had been overstated.

FORMATION OF QUALITY CIRCLES

Following the second phase of Circle Leader Training two Quality Circles formed immediately. The first of these consisted of nine members of the Administrative staff, two members of the teaching staff, and one member of the technician staff, and was led by a member of the administrative staff. Apart from one of the administrative staff members and one of the teaching staff members all were based on one college site.

The second Circle was composed entirely of Library Staff from all College sites comprising both professional and support staff. A third Quality Circle formed originally from a group of trained Circle Leaders soon consisted of two members of the teaching staff including one who acts as leader and seven members of the technician staff. These three circles formed soon after the completion of leader training in May, 1986. A fourth circle did not form until September, 1986, this was composed of 7 teaching staff in the Department of Business and Management Studies led by a member of staff who had undergone leader training.

No other Quality Circles have formed so far. Four trained leaders attended an initial meeting and two of them working together agreed to lead a Circle by recruiting amongst teaching staff who had already been approached and seemed keen. Nothing came of this because of:

> -Initial problems in finding a common time when staff could attend a meeting, along with problems in finding a free room at a time when staff were eventually available.

> -The most enthusiastic of the joint leaders was involved at short notice in organising some very large externally funded courses which took up all of her time.

OPERATION OF QUALITY CIRCLES

The Circle composed mainly of administrative staff initially chose a name by brainstorming and voting and decided on 'The Ever Decreasing Circle'. A booklet was produced giving details of Quality Circle procedures, as a training aid, and it was agreed that weekly meetings would be held until the techniques had been learned, following which they would be held every second week. A list of problems was generated and refined and the problem of lack of storage space was eventually decided on. Having brainstormed and defined the causes the circle constructed a cause and effect diagram and checklists for collection of data were drawn up. A number of other activities have been initiated by this Circle including questioning the Principal on why his annual staff development interviews only included members of the teaching staff and an initiative published in the weekly staff bulletin for a general spring clean and clear out of rubbish during the post-summer term administration week. The problem of storage space was eventually the subject of a management presentation in January, 1987 and the Circle moved on to consider its next problem of incorrect completion of enrolment forms.

The success of the presentation gave a great boost to the Circle. Membership has increased and the present problem is being tackled with great energy and determination. Data collection exercises and subsequent analysis have been very thorough. A survey of administrative procedures used in 40 Colleges outside Lancashire has been carried out and visits to all Lancashire Colleges have been arranged to interview Chief Administrative Officers and identify good practice. In addition two officers from County Hall have attended a Circle meeting to answer questions and clarify roles. The scope of the problem has inevitably widened and the final objectives for this exercise are now to develop greater administrative efficiency particularly in terms of links between teaching staff and the College administration and to promote a greater understanding by teaching staff of the importance of administrative procedures.

As a follow up to its presentation on storage space the Circle has initiated an annual competition for the tidiest staff workroom with the winner receiving a certificate. Any workroom winning the competition for two years running will be re-decorated!

The second circle composed of library staff also chose a name by brainstorming and voting. 'The Ideas Ad Lib Circle'. An agenda of problems was generated by brainstorming and a training manual was prepared. The first problem of overdue books was decided on and following the use of the standard Quality Circle techniques of brainstorming, cause and effect classification, data collection, and pareto analysis the major cause was found to be books borrowed by staff. A range of solutions were found and the problem was the subject of a management presentation in February, 1987. (See Appendix 1). One positive benefit following the presentation was an indication from the County Council that for the first time the College Library would be allowed to use money collected from staff and students in payment for lost library books to buy new stock. The circle is not meeting at present.

Both of these Circles have been able to implement several solutions to minor problems which haven't required a presentation to management, for example the standardisation of a number of administrative practices across College sites.

The third Quality Circle composed mainly of technician staff but led by a member of the teaching staff has now considered two major problems both of which have been the subjects of management presentations. The problems are Insurance and the external appearance of the College. Both presentations have been successful and action resulting has included clarification from the County Council on a number of insurance issues and the tidying up of certain parts of the College grounds including the provision of litter bins. This circle has proved successful in recruiting new members and is undergoing refresher training prior to considering its next problem. It has regularly made use of external specialists such as the Chief Caretaker, Chief Administrative Officer and Heads of Department to help with the problem solving process.

The fourth Quality Circle composed of members of teaching staff in the Business and Management Studies Department has related circle activity to a major curriculum problem, the operation of BTEC Courses. The Department has pursued a policy of a high level of integration in the operation of its BTEC National Course and as a result is wrestling with difficulties of resourcing, staff development, and timetabling, which are an inevitable consequence of new ways of working. The Circle, which has benefited from the membership of the Head of Department, has been careful to consult widely amongst non-members in the Department to verify its thinking on the issues via a questionnaire approach to data collection and while there has been no management presentation, as yet, some clear solutions are emerging which may prove a major challenge to College policies on issues such as allocation of teaching remission, resourcing of courses and cross departmental staff workrooms.

PROBLEMS RELATING TO THE OPERATION OF QUALITY CIRCLES

All Circles have proved relatively successful so far. A major problem, however, has been the reliance placed by members on the leaders in spite of the stressing of the key Quality Circles concept of everyone being responsible for progress. There has been a reluctance to recognise the fundamental point that while Quality Circles are potentially a very powerful force for initiating change which will benefit staff generally this process requires commitment and work outside of meetings for all members of the Quality Circle. The onus in data collection exercises, etc., has tended to fall on the Quality Circle Leaders even though a number of ways of involving other members of the Circles have been tried; such as asking a member to record a brainstorming session on the flip chart, or to re-cap a Quality Circle technique as a revision exercise for the Circle, or asking a member beforehand to raise a particular issue in a Quality Circle meeting.

All members of the teaching staff who attended Quality Circle Leader training found the techniques useful and agreed that these techniques would be helpful in the conduct of routine meetings. However, only one circle composed solely of teaching staff has been formed. Two reasons for this may be as follows:

> -A view persists that staff shouldn't be involved in solving management problems 'when there are people at a higher level than us, paid more, to solve problems for us'

> -A discussion paper produced by a group of senior departmental staff in mid 1986 identified the demands on staff time caused by what was seen as 'an illogical and haphazard College Committee Structure', combined with the demands of a team approach to many of the courses now being taught. In this context Quality Circles have been seen as an additional commitment that staff could well do without even though many existing meetings are recognised as being non productive. For example, all staff can give examples of meetings be they course team meetings, section meetings, academic board sub-committee meetings, academic board working party meetings, curriculum development meetings, which have disintegrated before the agenda has been worked through as several staff move onto the next meeting. Team approaches have been promoted by senior management as a means of democratising College procedures but

the frustration caused has disillusioned staff who perhaps need a more supportive framework. Quality Circles undoubtedly have the potential to relieve some of these frustrations by bringing a clearer procedure to the conduct of meetings, through the use of verteams, and a wider application of Quality Circle techniques.

Other problems have included a continuing distrust of the Principal's motives in promoting a Quality Circle programme. Teaching staff too have been suspicious of the consultant (support staff have overwhelmingly supported him). Certain incidents have not helped this situation:

> - When having solved the problem of storage space, the administrative staff circle found that a storeroom was suddenly converted to office accommodation without consulting them. This was no one's fault, being caused by a lack of communications, a lack of awareness of what the circle has been working on, and the fact that Quality Circles work outside the normal administrative and organisational structures. However, the Principal was blamed, the circle lost morale in the short term and one member left the circle altogether.

> - A supervisor involved in one circle was worried about the possible conflict of loyalties if as a circle member he disagreed with circle decisions and was then asked to implement them. The consultant advised him to leave the circle if he was worried by this; he did and was joined by a number of other circle members. The circle struggled on with a reduced membership. With hindsight it would have been better to advise the supervisor to remain in the circle but to be perfectly open at every stage about the conflict of interests and to use his experience to warn and advise the circle about the consequences of their actions.

A number of middle management staff have displayed a cynical attitude towards Quality Circles and have discouraged staff from attending by casting doubts on circle effectiveness. Staff have been told that Quality Circles mustn't interfere with their 'real' work. Often staff have been unable to attend Quality Circle meetings at the last minute because of 'urgent' departmental tasks. All of this points to the level of insecurity amongst middle managers caused by Quality Circle activity.

The summer holiday break in 1986 proved harmful to circle activity and because of the very busy enrolment period in the autumn term, the term was several weeks old before Quality Circle activity recommenced.

QUALITY CIRCLE MEMBER TRAINING, TRAINER TRAINING AND TRAINING FOR SENIOR STAFF IN QUALITY CIRCLE TECHNIQUES

In order to confront some of these problems a training programme was organised. Two member training courses were held in early September, 1986 which were designed to make members more aware of their role in Quality Circle activity. These courses were very useful in reinforcing the enthusiasm of Quality Circle members and proved an ideal launching pad for the Quality Circle programme after the summer break. They did, however, draw attention to a number of problems perceived by Circle members, in particular:

- Some circles were too large to make adequate progress

- Lack of progress was also caused by the need to learn the techniques thoroughly

- There was a need for Quality Circles to have successes which the whole College saw as important

- There was an urgency to make management presentations to maintain momentum, and if circles hadn't reached the point where solutions were forthcoming interim presentations should be made

- The lack of support from middle managers.

These views led to further training initiatives. The trainer training course was an attempt to ensure the future of Quality Circles and enhance the Quality of the programme by improving the skills of Quality Circle leaders. Also a number of key teaching staff were invited to learn Quality Circle techniques during this course. These staff weren't interested in Quality Circle membership but did want to use the techniques in other contexts. An important outcome of this course was the development of a procedure for conducting meetings via the use of Quality Circle techniques.

In March, 1987 the training course for senior staff was held. Participants included the Principal, Vice-Principals, Heads of Department, Chief Administrative Officer and a number of Senior Lecturers with cross College responsibilities. Following the course all of these staff recognised the power of the techniques to slow down the decision making process, make sure that all the options were considered and the right decision was made. A number of participants who had been very cynical about Quality Circles became much more supportive, even asking to attend meetings from time to time.

PRESENTATIONS/ACHIEVEMENTS OF QUALITY CIRCLES

As already stated all Quality Circles have been able to implement minor improvements in procedures without the need for management presentations and approvals. This has been particularly the case with the library staff circle and administrative staff circle where for the first time staff from different sites have been able to meet and compare ways of working. The Business Studies staff circle has benefited from the involvement of the Head of Department who has been able to implement minor changes suggested by the circle particularly relating to timetabling. Three circles have made presentations to management so far, the Administrative staff circle on the problem of storage space, the library circle on the problem of overdue books and the technician staff circle on insurance, and the external appearance of the College. In all cases circles have initially been reluctant to go through with the exercise and a great deal of practice and reassurance was required, but the presentations, which were all made to the Principal, have been highly professional, using flipcharts, overhead projectors, handbooks and photographs, all have been well received with clear outcomes in terms of action. They have provided a great boost to circle morale and in two cases have rejuvenated the circles concerned. Second presentations will no doubt prove easier, and will probably be made to the larger audience of the Heads of Department meeting. However, no recommendations so far have been in any way threatening to management. It will be interesting to see what happens when major college policies are questioned which may well be the case should be Business Studies Circle, as seems likely, recommend changes to systems of allocating remission and resources, and separate staff rooms for Business Studies staff, when the College policy is for mixed staff rooms.

MANAGEMENT AND ORGANISATION OF THE QUALITY CIRCLE PROGRAMME

During the period of the FEU project there have been four main aspects to this:

-The role of the Steering Committee

-The role of the Facilitator

-The role of the Co-ordinating Committee

-The relationship of the consultant to all of these.

The role of the Steering Committee

The Steering Committee has met four times during the life of the project representing a wide spectrum of opinion from both inside and outside the college. It has proved very useful in setting the overall aims of the project, relating the project to the general F.E. context, expressing and discussing opinions relevant to problems and difficulties facing the project, many of which have been of direct practical help, and generally keeping the project on course. The evaluation of the project has been much discussed during the later meetings of the Steering Committee, and the format of this monograph owes a great deal to the views of the members.

The role of the Facilitator

Could probably be summarised as follows:

-Co-ordinating the programme - by taking an overview - by being the single named person identified with the programme

-Administering the programme - ensuring that rooms, equipment, clerical help, etc., are available and that time is well used

-Helping to train members and leaders

-Communications and Publicity - ensuring that there is a high level of awareness about the programme throughout the College

-Source of information and support for Circle Leaders and members

-Enabling the progress of Circle work by 'oiling the wheels' where necessary

-Making policy decisions relating to the Quality Circle programme in negotiation with others, such as the consultant, or the co-ordinating committee, e.g. what issues can reasonably be dealt with by a Quality Circle, expansion or reduction of the programme

-Ensuring that key Quality Circle concepts are being observed, e.g. methodology, code of conduct

-Keeping records of Circle progress.

Support for Circle Leaders has been particularly important by acting as a 'resource' during Circle meetings, and meeting with Circle Leaders before meetings to prepare, and afterwards to review progress.

The role of the Co-ordinating Committee

Once a number of Quality Circles were established a Co-ordinating Committee was formed consisting of the Principal, one Head of Department, one Representative from Administrative Staff, one Representative from the College branch of NATFHE, all Quality Circle Leaders, one Representative from Technician Staff, one Representative from NALGO, and the Facilitator. The Consultant has been invited to all meetings which are held monthly.

Meetings have been well supported and have been particularly helpful in reviewing common problems facing Quality Circles and in giving support and encouragement to Circle Leaders. The terms of reference of the Committee include:

- Clarifying overall objectives and in particular determining which topics can be dealt with
- Drawing up implementation plans
- Ensuring adequate training arrangements
- Receiving reports from the Facilitator and Circle Leaders and responding to them
- Clarifying relationships between the work of Quality Circles and the work of the other groups in the College, e.g. Academic Board Sub-Committees
- Reviewing the progress of Quality Circles
- Advising on recognition of Circle achievements
- Where necessary, arranging for external consultancy help
- Advising on ways of evaluating Circle activities.

The role of the Consultant

The consultant's role has been determined by the needs of the programme. His first point of contact has been with the facilitator and the strengths that he has brought to the project have all been associated with his professional experience and expertise in initiating, maintaining and evaluating Quality Circle programmes. These qualities have been of benefit not only to the facilitator but also to Circle Leaders, Circle Members, Steering Committee and Co-ordinating Committee, since he has had a counselling, training and supportive function with all of these such as demonstrating a refinement of Quality Circle technique to a Circle struggling to make progress, or explaining to the Steering Committee how a particular difficulty might be resolved. Clearly since our experiment has been the first attempt to establish a Quality Circle programme in a College in this country it has also broken new ground for the consultant. His view, borne out in the literature, has been that in terms of staff attitudes, organisational ethos and style, difficulties encountered, and progress made there has been very little difference between our Quality Circle programme and programmes which he has established in other organisations. However, the marked differences in levels of acceptance of the programme between teaching staff and support staff may contradict this view with implications for the way in which Quality Circles are introduced into Colleges. This issue is discussed in the next chapter of this monograph.

Chapter 3

EVALUATION OF THE PROGRAMME

Monitoring of the work of Quality Circles is an ongoing process. Each Quality Circle meeting is clerked and a brief report is filed, so that there is an official record of progress. Monitoring also takes place via contacts between the Facilitator and Circle Leaders, through the work of the Co-ordinating Committee, through the overview taken by the Steering Committee and through the presentations to Management made by each Circle. The Steering Committee in the course of its meetings decided that evaluation of the project should be on the basis of:

- The level of achievement of the four aims stated in the original project proposal (See Page 33)

- The level of achievement of the Principal's expectations of the project (See Page 34)

- The level and achievements of benefits anticipated by the group of opinion formers interviewed in the first phase of the project (listed below)

- the continuation of a Quality Circle programme beyond the life of the project.

BENEFITS ANTICIPATED BY OPINION FORMERS

Following the original presentations about Quality Circles to all staff a group of key staff (senior managers, Heads of functions, etc.) were interviewed and listed the following as benefits they hoped for from a Quality Circles programme:

- To provide a channel for showing that the voices of the lower levels can be heard

- To help my staff become more involved in a managing role

- To make teachers more familiar with obstacles outside the College, e.g. at County Hall

- To give training in decision making techniques
- To promote greater staff commitment
- To help generate more participation
- To promote greater efficiency in running laboratories
- To disseminate information on new courses
- To give more real understanding of other peoples problems
- To remove the sense of isolation felt in the classroom
- To provide opportunities to learn more about administration and management
- To provide recognition that every individual is equally important in the organisation
- To improve morale and efficiency
- To improve co-operation between different departments
- To help people with common interests identify more closely with each other
- To help team work
- To give staff a better idea of how the college is run
- To include administrative and ancillary staff earlier in discussions
- To help morale and communications
- To improve participation
- To improve the quality of work at the chalk face
- To improve communication between sites
- To improve the College's sense of direction
- To give more feedback from the grass roots
- To improve insights for Management into problems
- To recognise long service amongst administrative staff

-To improve dialogue because of the voluntary nature of the Circles

-To bring to light issues which wouldn't otherwise have emerged

-To involve people who would otherwise not be involved

-To improve the quality of decisions

DRAWING UP OF THE QUESTIONNAIRE

The view of the Steering Committee was that evaluation should be on the basis of a questionnaire drawn up in relation to these stated benefits which touch upon a broad range of topics including communications, team, development, involvement in or better understanding of management, participation, commitment, efficiency, effectiveness, and quality of work. The resulting questionnaire (below) was piloted and administered by post to one in five staff, and face to face with the original opinion formers, and Quality Circle Leaders.

THE QUESTIONNAIRE: FINAL DRAFT FOLLOWING PILOTING

PLEASE PLACE A TICK IN THE BOX WHICH YOU
FEEL IS THE CLOSEST TO YOUR OWN VIEW

1. (i) How do you rate communications in the College?

	Very Good	Good	Neither good nor bad	Bad	Very Bad
In your Department					
Between Departments					
Between Sites					
College as a whole					

Please comment on your ratings here:

(ii) Do you feel that Quality Circles either already have, or will, in the future, improve communications?

Please tick a box from 1 to 7 to show what you think is the degree of effect which Quality Circles have had or might have in the future. For example, if you think that Quality Circles have had "no effect" you should place a tick under box 1. If you think that Quality Circles have brought about a "very marked improvement" or might do in the future you should place a tick under box 7. If you feel that the effect of Quality Circles is or might be somewhere between "No effect" and "very marked improvement" please tick a box between 2 and 6 to indicate your view

	No Effect	1	2	3	4	5	6	7	Very marked improvement
At this moment									
In the future									

(iii) If you feel able to, please give an example to illustrate your ratings:

_____
_____

2. (i) What are your observations on the quality of team work in the College?

	Very Good	Good	Neither good nor bad	Bad	Very Bad
In your Department					
The College as a whole					

Please comment on your ratings here:
_____
_____

(ii) Do you feel that Quality Circles either already have, or will, in the future improve team working?

	No Effect	1	2	3	4	5	6	7	Very marked improvement
At this moment									
In the future									

(iii) Please comment on this with an example, if possible.
_____
_____

3. (i) To what extent do you feel that staff have a sense of involvement in the running (i.e. organisation, administration, management) of the College?

Very much involved	Significantly involved	Just about involved	Not at all involved

Please comment on your ratings here:
_____
_____

(ii) Do you feel that Quality Circles either already have, or will, in the future, improve staff involvement in the running (i.e. organisation administration, management) of the College?

	No Effect	1	2	3	4	5	6	7	Very marked improvement
At this moment									
In the future									

4. (i) How do you rate efficiency and effectiveness in the College?

Very High	High	Neither high nor low	Low	Very Low

Please comment on your rating here:
_____
_____

(ii) Would you please describe an aspect of College life that you consider to be particularly efficient and/or effective:
_____
_____

(iii) Do you feel that Quality Circles either already have, or will, in the future, improve efficiency and effectiveness?

	No Effect	1	2	3	4	5	6	7	Very marked improvement
At this moment									
In the future									

(iv) Please comment on this with an example, if possible.
_____
_____

(i) What does the expression "quality of work" mean to you in the College context?
_____
_____

(ii) What action, if any, would be needed to improve the quality of work done in the College?
_____
_____

(iii) How do you rate the quality of work done in the College?

Very High	High	Neither high nor low	Low	Very Low

Please comment on your rating here:
_____
_____

(iv) Do you feel that Quality Circles either already have, or will, in the future, improve the quality of work in the College?

	No Effect	1	2	3	4	5	6	7	Very marked improvement
At this moment									
In the future									

6. (i) What do the expressions "curriculum" and "curriculum issues" mean to you?
_____
_____

(ii) To what extent do you feel involved in the development and provision of the curriculum?

Very much involved	Significantly involved	Just about involved	Not at all involved

(iii) Would you wish for a greater involvement – if so in what way would you wish to become more involved?
_____
_____

(iv) Do you think Quality Circles culd have an influence on the curriuclum and related issues – if so, in what way?
_____
_____
_____

7. Are there any other comments you wish to make on the Quality Circle programme?
_____
_____

8. If a further one day appreciation course on Quality Circle techniques were to be held at a time convenient to you, would you wish to participate?
_____

9. Are you a member of a Quailty Circle? If so, please indicate how you feel about the experience.
_____
_____

Thank you for your co-operation in completing this questionnaire.
Your views will be most helpful.

ANALYSIS OF THE QUESTIONAIRE

The questionnaire was distributed to one in five staff simply by taking every fifth name from a complete staff list. The questionnaires were colour coded into the following categories of staff:- Senior Management, Heads of Department, Senior Lecturers, Lecturers, and Support Staff, other than this they were anonymous.

Questions related to communications, quality of team work, sense of involvement in the running (i.e. organisation, administration and management) of the College, efficiency and effectiveness, quality of work, curriculum, and the current potential effects of the Quality Circle programme on all of these. An indication of the cynicism shown by lecturers towards the Quality Circle programme was the volume of questionnaires returned which was as follows:

Senior Management 100%, Heads of Department 100%, Senior Lecturers 100%, Lecturers 25%, Support Staff 35%. Percentages given in the statistical tables relating to the questionnaire responses relate to questionnaires returned, not the number issued.

Communications in the College

In the Senior Management Category communications in the College were rated as average to poor with most problems arising from the split site nature of the College and from perceived or real hierarchies (Table 1 & 2). It was thought that Quality Circles had already significantly improved communications because of staff, particularly support staff, meeting for the first time to discuss common problems. The potential of Quality Circles to improve communications in the future was rated as very high. Amongst Heads of Department it was felt that communications within departments was generally good, between departments neither good nor bad, between sites on the whole poor, and in the College as a whole average. Particular problems cited were the split site nature of the College and departmental staff based in 'mixed' workrooms. There was general optimism about both the current effect of Quality Circles on communications and the ability of Quality Circles to improve communications in the future.

One commented:

"Circle meetings have made me more aware of the difficulties sub-groups have in continuing once they have been formed unless a determined effort is made to make meetings run well by involving the whole group."

All Senior Lecturers felt that communications in their own departments were good but between departments and between College sites they were average to poor. Opinion was divided on communications in the College as a whole, an equal number feeling that they were both good and bad. The split site nature of

Table 1
How do you rate communications in the College?

		Very Good %	Good %	Neither Good nor Bad %	Bad %	Very Bad %	Total %
	Senior Management	–	?	–	–	–	–
	Heads of Dept.	33	33	33	–	–	100
In	Senior Lecturers	–	100	–	–	–	100
Your	Lecturers	–	29	43	14	14	100
Dept.	Support Staff	–	50	34	16	–	100
	Opinion Formers	20	50	20	10	–	100
	QC Leaders/Members	–	20	60	20	–	100
	Senior Management	–	–	–	–	–	–
	Heads of Dept.	–	33	33	33	–	100
Between	Senior Lecturers	–	–	50	50	–	100
Depts.	Lecturers	–	–	29	71	–	100
	Support Staff	–	16	67	17	–	100
	Opinion Formers	20	10	50	20	–	100
	QC Leaders/Members	–	20	–	80	–	100
	Senior Management	–	–	–	100	–	100
	Heads of Dept.	–	–	33	66	–	100
Between	Senior Lecturers	–	–	50	25	25	100
Sites	Lecturers	–	–	15	42	43	100
	Support Staff	–	16	50	34	–	100
	Opinion Formers	10	20	30	40	–	100
	QC Leaders/Members	–	–	40	60	–	100
	Senior Management	–	–	100	–	–	100
In	Heads of Dept.	–	–	66	33	–	100
the	Senior Lecturers	–	50	–	50	–	100
College	Lecturers	–	14	14	58	14	100
as a	Support Staff	–	16	50	34	–	100
whole	Opinion Formers	–	40	40	20	–	100
	QC Leaders/Members	–	–	20	60	20	100

Table 2
Do you feel that Quality Circles either already have or will in the future improve communications?

		% No Effect	(%) 1	(%) 2	(%) 3	(%) 4	(%) 5	(%) 6	(%) 7	Very marked Improvement %	Total %
At this Moment	Senior Management	-	-	-	100	-	-	-	-	-	100
	Heads of Dept.	33	-	-	33	-	33	-	-	-	100
	Senior Lecturers	25	50	25	-	-	-	-	-	-	100
	Lecturers	29	71	-	-	-	-	-	-	-	100
	Support Staff	16	50	-	17	17	-	-	-	-	100
	Opinion Formers	10	-	20	10	10	10	20	-	10	90
	QC Leaders/Members	-	-	-	60	20	-	-	-	-	80
In the Future	Senior Management	-	-	-	-	-	-	-	100	-	100
	Heads of Dept.	-	33	-	-	-	33	-	33	-	100
	Senior Lecturers	-	50	-	-	50	-	-	-	-	100
	Lecturers	14	14	14	14	-	-	-	-	14	100
	Support Staff	-	50	-	-	-	33	17	-	-	100
	Opinion Formers	-	-	10	-	30	20	10	-	-	70
	QC Leaders/Members	-	-	-	20	20	20	-	-	-	60

the College was seen as the main source of communications problems. Improvements to communications brought about by Quality Circles were so far seen as marginal. They were seen to provide an opportunity for the future but there was a view that management might not be inclined to implement circle suggestions.

Lecturers generally rated communications in their own departments as being neither good nor bad and between departments, between sites and in the College as a whole as being generally bad. The split site nature of the College was again seen as the main difficulty leading to the late arrival of letters and information, but there was also criticism of impolite memos, letters going astray, misunderstandings about the aims and objectives of various courses with little co-operation and 'entrenched departmental interests' preventing real communication on central issues. A majority felt that Quality Circles would have a minimal effect on communications although one felt that with adequate resources Quality Circles could lead to a 'very marked improvement'. Others felt that any improvements would come via the hierarchical structure of Senior Management, Heads of Department and Senior Lecturers. A majority of support staff felt that communications in their own department were good, between departments and in the College as a whole were average, but between College sites were poor. Most felt that Quality Circles while not having a great impact on communications at present might do so in the future since they had been successful in industry. As one respondent succinctly put it:

"The closer to people you are the better the communication."

Quality of Teamwork in the College

The senior management view on the quality of team work in the College was that it was good and improving as a result of a more integrated curriculum. The Quality Circle amongst Business Studies staff was seen to have already improved team working, and the process would continue once further circles of teaching staff were formed.

Amongst Heads of Department there were mixed views about the quality of team work in the College some feeling that on balance it was very good while some felt that many College teams had no clear function repeatedly looking at issues without ever finding solutions. It was felt that Quality Circles could improve this situation by benefiting staff who generally work alone and also that non Quality Circle teams could learn from the discipline and techniques of Quality Circle activity. It was also thought that delegated responsibility via Quality Circles would produce results.

A majority of Senior Lecturers felt that team work in their own Departments was good but in the College as a whole was bad.

Table 3
What are your observations on the Quality of Team work in the College?

		Very Good %	Good %	Neither Good nor Bad %	Bad %	Very Bad %	Total %
In Your Dept.	Senior Management	–	–	–	–	–	–
	Heads of Dept.	33	33	33	–	–	100
	Senior Lecturers	50	25	25	–	–	100
	Lecturers	43	–	43	14	–	100
	Support Staff	–	67	17	16	–	100
	Opinion Formers	40	40	10	–	–	100
	QC Leaders/Members	20	20	40	20	–	100
In the College as a whole	Senior Management	–	100	–	–	–	100
	Heads of Dept.	–	–	66	33	–	100
	Senior Lecturers	25	–	25	50	–	100
	Lecturers	–	–	43	57	–	100
	Support Staff	–	–	84	16	–	100
	Opinion Formers	–	50	50	–	–	100
	QC Leaders/Members	–	20	80	–	–	100

Table 4
Do you feel that Quality Circles either already have or will, in the future, improve team working?

		% No Effect	(%) 1	(%) 2	(%) 3	(%) 4	(%) 5	(%) 6	(%) 7	Very marked Improvement %	Total %
At this Moment	Senior Management	–	–	–	–	100	–	–	–	–	100
	Heads of Dept.	33	–	–	–	33	33	–	–	–	100
	Senior Lecturers	–	75	25	–	–	–	–	–	–	100
	Lecturers	29	57	14	–	–	–	–	–	–	100
	Support Staff	16	50	17	17	–	–	–	–	–	100
	Opinion Formers	20	10	10	–	20	–	10	–	10	80
	QC Leaders/Members	–	–	40	–	20	–	–	20	–	80
In the Future	Senior Management	–	–	–	–	–	–	–	100	–	100
	Heads of Dept.	–	–	–	–	33	–	33	33	–	100
	Senior Lecturers	–	50	25	–	–	25	–	–	–	100
	Lecturers	14	14	29	15	–	–	–	–	–	100
	Support Staff	–	16	33	–	–	51	–	–	–	100
	Opinion Formers	–	–	–	–	40	10	10	10	–	70
	QC Leaders/Members	–	–	20	–	–	40	–	–	–	60

There was a view that teams worked better as democratic units although this wasn't defined. The point was made that relatively few people were involved in Quality Circles, but they did augur well for the development of a team approach to problems.

Most lecturers agreed that team work was very good in Departments but poor in the College as a whole, the major problem again being the split site nature of the College. Some individuals who were conscientious were seen to operate well as team leaders but this tended to be in spite of lack of support 'from above'. Their success was due to

"The feeling of loyalty of one lecturer to another, not necessarily loyalty to the department or the College".

It was felt that Quality Circles could improve team working on cross college issues but a majority of lecturers were uncertain as to the present or future benefits of Quality Circles.

Regarding the quality of team work most support staff felt that this was good within their own departments and average in the College as a whole. One person pointed to a lack of interest amongst support staff and the difficulties of promoting a team approach when an organisation is so large. There was a view that Quality Circles were capable of changing attitudes and improving team working, but there wasn't enough interest in Quality Circles, and Quality Circle methods took too long. Results were often required more quickly.

Sense of involvement in the Running of the College (i.e. organisation, administration, management)

Senior Management felt that staff were already significantly involved in the running of the College but that

"while most staff acknowledged that they had a bureaucratic role to play few identified with the purposes of bureaucracy".

The Senior Management view was that Quality Circles had already significantly increased staff involvement in the running of the College and would further do so in the future. A majority of Heads of Department felt that staff were 'just about involved' in the running of the College. All felt that Quality Circles would improve this situation in the future. Most Senior Lecturers felt that they were 'just about involved' in the running of the College. However, they didn't really feel influential because of external factors and although there was a highly developed structure for consulting them, their views weren't really taken into account and there was no real devolution of executive power:

"We have a deplorable system. Committees duplicate each other and no-one knows if reports are even seriously considered"

"Staff may feel involved, but there are so many factors we are unaware of that I wonder just how involved we really are"

"Academic board is a sham! It represents no-one but the people on it".

While it was felt that Quality Circles had already had some impact on this situation and had further potential, there was no guarantee that they could exert influence in a way that College committees often failed to do, and their recommendations might be ignored.

Table 5

To what extent do you feel that staff have a sense of involvement in the running (i.e. organisation, administration, management) of the College?

	Very much involved %	Significantly involved %	Just about involved %	Not at all involved %	Total %
Senior Management	–	100	–	–	100
Heads of Dept.	–	33	66	–	100
Senior Lecturers	–	25	75	–	100
Lecturers	–	14	58	14	86
Support Staff	–	–	66	34	100
Opinion Formers	–	40	30	20	90
QC Leaders/Members	–	20	60	20	100

Table 6

Do you feel that Quality Circles either already have, or will in the future, improve staff involvement in the running (i.e. organisation, administration, management) of the College?

		% No Effect	(%) 1	(%) 2	(%) 3	(%) 4	(%) 5	(%) 6	(%) 7	Very marked Improvement %	Total %
At this Moment	Senior Management	–	–	–	100	–	–	–	–	–	100
	Heads of Dept.	33	–	33	–	–	33	–	–	–	100
	Senior Lecturers	25	50	25	–	–	–	–	–	–	100
	Lecturers	29	71	–	–	–	–	–	–	–	100
	Support Staff	34	34	16	16	–	–	–	–	–	100
	Opinion Formers	–	10	10	20	10	10	10	10	–	80
	QC Leaders/Members	–	–	20	60	–	–	–	–	–	80
In the Future	Senior Management	–	–	–	–	–	–	–	100	–	100
	Heads of Dept.	–	33	–	–	33	–	33	–	–	100
	Senior Lecturers	–	75	–	–	–	25	–	–	–	100
	Lecturers	14	29	14	15	–	–	–	–	–	72
	Support Staff	–	–	17	33	17	16	17	–	–	100
	Opinion Formers	–	–	–	10	10	10	20	20	–	70
	QC Leaders/Members	–	–	20	20	–	–	20	–	–	60

Most lecturers felt just about involved in the running of the College but were highly critical:

"Involvement is there but no-one ever comes back to grass roots to see if the decisions made have eased the work load or made more work. Too many chiefs not enough Indians!"

"Too much 'lip service' is paid to involvement, too many committees and too much talking without seeing great changes. People are interested and involved initially but then feel disillusioned."

There was also some resentment about the role of a few 'chosen people' who seemed to be involved in everything. One lecturer maintained that staff felt manipulated and many saw Quality Circles as a means not of improving staff involvement in the running of the College but simply as a device to increase the manipulation of staff:

"Most Staff voice the opinion that they are treated like menials and only used as pawns. We feel manipulated."

66% of support staff respondents felt just about involved in the running of the College. The remainder felt not at all involved. There was seen to be too great a gap between management and the rest. Decisions were made and forced upon staff without having been thought through properly. One person felt that support staff weren't encouraged to feel involved in the running of the College. All felt that Quality Circles could only improve the current situation.

Efficiency and Effectiveness in the College

It was felt by Senior Management that the College was already efficient and effective on most current indicators of performance such as class sizes, but the Quality Circles would increasingly contribute to this process since when people are involved with and committed to an institution they begin to suggest and implement more efficient and effective methods of operation.

Heads of Department generally rated efficiency and effectiveness in the College as being below average. Some parts of the College were thought to be much more efficient than others and one comment ran:

"The work output is great but the level of achievement is exemplified by the (resulting) chaos. The motto should be "attempt less, achieve more!"."

A number of areas of work thought to be efficient and effective were cited notably performing arts events, special needs provision and the College Training Restaurant. It was also thought that the College was good at developing new initiatives such as CPVE and creche provision. Quality Circles were seen to have a role in improving efficiency and effectiveness particularly administrative efficiency.

A majority of Senior Lecturers agreed that the College was efficient and effective and that this was reflected in its reputation and results. There was uncertainty, however, over what was meant by effectiveness and efficiency which were vague terms. There was concern about bureaucracy, lack of information, co-ordination and planning. The teaching function and the library were given as examples of particularly efficient and effective aspects of the College life. There was some appreciation of administrative problems already solved by Quality Circles leading to greater efficiency but it was generally felt that the scale of the Quality Circle programme was too small to be influential.

Most lecturers rated the efficiency and effectiveness of the College as low but they defined this as being management and administration. Criticisms included too many requests for the same information, the problems caused by split sites, and constant non-availability of key people:

"Due to poor communications and split sites people try hard and care but are constantly thwarted".

It was felt that teaching staff were effective but the management standard was poor:

"Individuals are in general very effective teachers, most problems are created by the so called leaders who then make a great show of how hard they are working to put matters right."

"The low end of the College staff is carrying upper management and doing well in spite of them - not because of them."

It was thought by some that Quality Circles could solve specific problems such as postal communications, minibus services, student facilities, organisation, and the use of resources, but others were less confident:

"Quality Circles will not be able to provide the resources (rooms, equipment, attitudes) necessary to improve efficiency/effectiveness."

and one person was downright dismissive:

"I do not take them seriously and have yet to find anyone else who does apart from Tim Atkinson and the Principal."

There was at least some comfort for me:

"Don't take it personal Tim. I know why you're doing it."

With this comment the respondent showed that he or she was wiser than I was!

Table 7
How do you rate efficiency and effectiveness in the College?

	Very High %	High %	Neither High nor Low %	Low %	Very Low %	Total %
Senior Management	–	100	–	–	–	100
Heads of Dept.	–	–	33	66	–	100
Senior Lecturers	–	50	25	25	–	100
Lecturers	–	–	14	71	–	85
Support Staff	–	–	67	33	–	100
Opinion Formers	–	50	40	–	–	90
QC Leaders/Members	–	40	60	–	–	100

Table 8
Do you feel that Quality Circles either already have or will in the future improve efficiency and effectiveness?

		% No Effect	(%) 1	(%) 2	(%) 3	(%) 4	(%) 5	(%) 6	(%) 7	Very marked Improvement %	Total %
At this Moment	Senior Management	–	–	–	100	–	–	–	–	–	100
	Heads of Dept.	33	–	66	–	–	–	–	–	–	100
	Senior Lecturers	–	75	25	–	–	–	–	–	–	100
	Lecturers	29	43	–	14	–	–	–	–	–	86
	Support Staff	17	50	–	33	–	–	–	–	–	100
	Opinion Formers	20	10	10	10	–	10	10	–	–	70
	QC Leaders/Members	–	–	20	40	–	20	–	–	–	90
In the Future	Senior Management	–	–	–	–	–	–	–	100	–	100
	Heads of Dept.	–	33	–	–	33	33	–	–	–	100
	Senior Lecturers	–	50	–	–	25	25	–	–	–	100
	Lecturers	14	29	14	–	14	–	–	–	–	71
	Support Staff	–	16	16	17	–	34	17	–	–	100
	Opinion Formers	–	–	–	10	10	30	20	–	–	70
	QC Leaders/Members	–	–	–	20	–	20	20	–	–	60

The majority of support staff rated efficiency and effectiveness in the College as average to low although catering courses particularly and students results generally were seen as examples of College life which were particularly successful. It was felt that problems of size and the split site nature of the College did not make for efficiency and effectiveness and that standards varied in different parts of the College. All felt, to varying degrees, that Quality Circles had a contribution to make to the efficiency and effectiveness of the College.

Quality of Work in the College

The Senior Management view of what constituted 'Quality of Work' (Table 9 & 10) in the College context was that it related to the student experience supported by the staff experience and could be improved by a clearer understanding of the aims and objectives of the College, a universal adoption of these, and improved resources (human, temporal and financial) to achieve them. It was thought that the quality of work done in the College was already rated highly by the LEA, competitors, and users, and that Quality Circles were already contributing to the quality of work done in the College and would do so, increasingly, in the future.

Heads of Department interpreted the question on quality of work in the College in different ways, some relating it to the service given to students, particularly through the method of delivery. Others interpreted it on a personal basis, considering that tasks allocated needed to be appropriate to the role of the individual and within his or her powers to accomplish. There was a general

Table 9
How do you rate the quality of work done in the College?

	Very High %	High %	Neither High nor Low %	Low %	Very Low %	Total %
Senior Management	–	100	–	–	–	100
Heads of Dept.	–	33	66	–	–	100
Senior Lecturers	25	50	25	–	–	100
Lecturers	–	71	29	–	–	100
Support Staff	–	34	66	–	–	100
Opinion Formers	10	70	20	–	–	100
QC Leaders/Members	–	60	20	–	–	80

Table 10
Do you feel that Quality Circles either already have or will, in the future, improve the quality of work in the College?

		% No Effect	(%) 1	(%) 2	(%) 3	(%) 4	(%) 5	(%) 6	(%) 7	Very marked Improvement %	Total %
At this Moment	Senior Management	–	–	–	100	–	–	–	–	–	100
	Heads of Dept.	33	–	33	33	–	–	–	–	–	100
	Senior Lecturers	25	50	25	–	–	–	–	–	–	100
	Lecturers	29	58	–	–	–	–	–	–	–	87
	Support Staff	33	50	17	–	–	–	–	–	–	100
	Opinion Formers	20	10	10	10	10	10	–	–	–	70
	QC Leaders/Members	–	–	40	20	–	20	–	–	–	80
In the Future	Senior Management	–	–	–	–	–	–	–	100	–	100
	Heads of Dept.	–	33	–	–	–	33	33	–	–	100
	Senior Lecturers	25	25	25	–	–	25	–	–	–	100
	Lecturers	14	29	29	–	–	–	–	–	–	72
	Support Staff	–	17	17	33	33	–	–	–	–	100
	Opinion Formers	–	–	–	20	10	20	10	–	–	60
	QC Leaders/Members	–	20	–	–	–	20	20	–	–	60

feeling that quality of work would be improved by clearer definitions of staff responsibilities and by concentrating rather more on teaching/learning aspects of current programmes than 'kite flying'. The majority view was that the quality of work done in the College was neither high nor low, staff generally seeing some parts of their job as being more important than others, many for example rating teaching above administration. There was a general view that Quality Circles were already improving the quality of work done in the College and would do so to a greater extent in the future.

The views of Senior Lecturers on what constitutes 'Quality of Work' in the College context were stated in different ways, but all related to the promotion of a happy and successful student experience through high standards of teaching, effective support staff, and adequate funding. It was felt that Quality of work would be improved by more resources including specialised classrooms and workshops, more support staff (so that teachers could devote all of their time to teaching), better staff conditions, particularly workrooms, 'people orientated' leadership and less bureaucratic management. More staff training was needed to cope with the greater variety of students now attending college. In spite of these difficulties a majority of Senior Lecturers rated the quality of work done in the College as high. Students were thought to benefit and enjoy their experience at the College.

"I consider the quality of work is high when one looks at the progress of most of our students who once they leave College fulfil a useful happy and well adjusted role

in society. This is not easy in the world today but when one meets students in later life their time here is always spoken of with pride."

There was perhaps a hint of complacency in some of the views expressed:

"In spite of the difficulties the College has a generally motivated, dedicated and talented staff and good students."

Quality Circles were generally thought to have already contributed to the quality of work done with the potential for doing so to a greater extent in the future.

Lecturers gave a number of definitions of what they meant by 'quality of work' all of which related to the teaching/learning process and two of which are worth quoting in full:

"The feeling that one is making a significant contribution, ultimately for the benefit of the students"

"It is seeing that the process of learning is as important as the product and having time to provide a responsive environment for students, to build relationships with work placement providers, part time, and servicing staff in order to develop courses"

To improve the quality of work done in the College it was thought that unnecessary administration for teaching staff should be eliminated, and that there should be less movement between sites for both staff and students. There should be a greater recognition of classroom activity as the central role of the College with teaching excellence rewarded by promotions which at present were given to people for what were seen as peripheral activities. In spite of these comments, most lecturers felt that the quality of work done in the College was high owing to the commitment of staff whose morale was often low because they felt their work was not appreciated. It was thought that Quality Circles at present were having little effect on quality of work, but they would do to an increasing extent in the future. Support staff saw 'quality of work' in the College context as being a high overall standard shown by examination results, student enthusiasm and good, well run courses. One person added:

"In the context of my own work the best job that can be done with the tools provided".

A majority felt that the quality of work done in the College was average and could be improved by changes in attitude. Quality Circles were one way to achieve this and had the potential to do so in the future.

Curriculum and Curriculum Issues

Expressions 'curriculum' and 'curriculum issues' were defined by senior management as being 'The student experience, taught and untaught and matters related to that experience'. There was a feeling of significant involvement in the development of the curriculum and a view that Quality Circles could have an influence on the curriculum and related issues. In fact, since curriculum was such a central issue it would be a theme running through most Quality Circles. The deliberations and proposals of Quality Circles were bound to affect curriculum anyway.

Heads of Department saw curriculum as being

"the means by which we educate and train via the organisation of courses".

Curriculum issues were seen as

"our priorities in improving the education and training of students".

A majority of Heads of Department felt very much involved in the development and provision of the curriculum. One Head of Department indicated that he wanted to be involved to a greater extent by looking at ways in which subjects offered in his department could be integrated into a cross College curriculum. There was a general view that Quality Circles could have an influence on curriculum related issues through an analysis of problems of delivery and teaching problems generally. One Head of Department felt that they were a way of involving the local community in curriculum development.

Curriculum was defined by Senior Lecturers as being the whole concept of a course of study 'what we teach, how we teach, who we teach, for what end, and with what success'. Curriculum issues were seen as individual aspects of this, such as methods of assessment, entry qualifications, methodology. All Senior Lecturers felt sufficiently involved in the curriculum but were aware of the possibilities for becoming more involved as members of regional subject panels or examination boards. One felt he or she could become more involved but:

"Only by giving me more hours in the day, but I think I'm entitled to a rest"

There was a view that Quality Circles could have an influence on the curriculum if they were based on subject or section groupings of staff. It was acknowledged, however, that staff didn't seem inclined to work in this way.

Curriculum was considered by lecturers to be course design and evaluation, and the substance of what is taught, who is taught along with how the teaching takes place. Curriculum issues were seen to be any aspect of this process such as aims, objectives, content, method, organisation, resources and evaluation. Most lecturers felt 'just about involved' in the development and provision of the curriculum, but only one felt very much involved. A number wished for a greater involvement but saw problems in this, notably time constraints caused by split site working and difficulties in pulling course teams together. There was some scepticism over the ability to influence management through a greater involvement:

"I would like upper management to listen to all staff, not just the 'Yes' people".

Most lecturers felt that Quality Circles could have little effect on curriculum issues except in the areas of organisation and support services and one made the comment:

"Like communism, very desirable in theory - a joke in practice".

Support staff defined curriculum and curriculum issues in a wide sense as courses of study in a College and anything related to College activities. A majority of support staff felt that they were not at all involved in curriculum issues although one felt just about involved and perhaps surprisingly one felt very much involved. They generally felt that curriculum issues were not applicable to them. One person didn't want a greater involvement but felt that more knowledge of curriculum issues would make for better communication and understanding. Most support staff felt that Quality Circles could have an influence on the curriculum and related issues by giving more people a clearer picture of College 'aims'. It was also thought that more involvement could lead to greater efficiency. There was a view that only teaching staff should be involved in Quality Circles looking at curriculum issues.

Table 11
To what extent do you feel involved in the development and provision of the curriculum?

	Very much involved %	Significantly involved %	Just about involved %	Not at all involved %	Total %
Senior Management	–	100	–	–	100
Heads of Dept.	66	–	33	–	100
Senior Lecturers	25	75	–	–	100
Lecturers	14	29	57	–	100
Support Staff	17	–	17	66	100
Opinion Formers	20	20	30	30	100
QC Leaders/Members	40	–	40	20	100

General Comments

Senior Management felt that Quality Circles were a welcome development but more active participation was necessary. Heads of Department felt that Quality

Circles were a good way of finding solutions to problems, but took too long. Most problems didn't need an 'ideal' solution and by focussing on one problem over a period of time, more urgent, pressing problems might be ignored.

The success of Quality Circles amongst support staff was noted by Senior Lecturers, one raising the issue of whether support staff had more time, could more easily attend meetings, were keener than teaching staff or more aware of problems. The point was made that Quality Circle techniques were valuable, and might well expedite Committee work but they needed a membership with common interests and were not appropriate for cross college issues. A number said they would attend Quality Circles if they were allocated time to attend. There was a view that management expertise should have been used to improve existing systems rather than create parallel ones and that the money spent on Quality Circles would have been more effectively spent elsewhere. 75% of Senior Lecturers who completed the questionnaire were keen to attend further Quality Circle training courses.

Responses to this question from Lecturers indicated that a number of them were unaware of circle progress and achievements. There was some resentment about the way they were 'thrust upon' the College. One person was keen to be involved in Quality Circle activity but felt that this would be at the expense of students interests. Interestingly, one lecturer who had undergone Quality Circle leader training was not involved in the circle programme but was benefiting from the use of the techniques. 43% of those lecturers who completed the questionnaire were interested in Quality Circle training should the opportunity arise.

There was a view amongst support staff that circles only worked if the problem being considered was small enough to be resolved fairly quickly, and that management presentations were an important feature which must take place regularly. A majority of the support staff completing the questionnaire were interested in attending further Quality Circle training courses.

INTERVIEWS WITH ORIGINAL OPINION FORMERS AND QUALITY CIRCLE PARTICIPANTS

As part of the evaluation process the Consultant interviewed a group of the original opinion formers, whose anticipated benefits of Quality Circles had been listed at the start of the project, together with a group of quality circle participants. The questionnaire already used was the basis of the interviews and was completed by each person interviewed. The consultant was also seeking to gain information on what these groups saw as achievements/benefits, obstacles/constraints, management support and future development, and wrote a commentary on the progress of the interviews dealing particularly with these issues.

Opinion Formers Group Questionnaire Responses

Views on communications tended to reflect the views of the wider group of staff surveyed although a significant minority rated them as very good both within and between departments and this was the only group from which anyone rated communications between sites as being very good. Also this group revealed some interesting additional ideas such as that some sections had traditionally been isolated but seemed to prefer it that way. There was an appreciation of the need for more cross college committees and working groups to aid communications but concern that this then made the chain of command unclear. The general view was that Quality Circles were bound to improve communications because of their very nature but one person made the point that:

"The effect was good at the beginning, but less so now".

The quality of team work in the College was thought to be high and that Quality Circles were contributing to this already and would potentially do so to a greater extent, although one person said that:

"The idea of Quality Circles is completely foreign to the Department"

The urgency of the new curricular activities in demanding cross departmental groupings of staff was mentioned and one person pointed to the efforts made by full time staff to involve part-time teachers in course teams. As might be expected most of this group felt significantly involved in the running of the College but were concerned that there was a gulf between management and staff. One person felt that there were already opportunities for other staff within the College to become more involved, but these weren't always fully utilised. Quality Circles were seen to be already improving this situation and were likely to do so to a far greater extent in the future. It was felt that teaching staff saw themselves as more involved in curriculum management.

While efficiency and effectiveness were already rated highly there were specific examples of areas where drastic improvements were required, such as publicity. Quality Circles were seen to have a future role to play in improving efficiency and effectiveness but staff didn't see them as an integral part of the process pointing out that they would have to leave work undone so that they could go to Quality Circle meetings. One person said:

"It's just not practical to find the time"

Many examples were given of aspects of college life which were particularly efficient and effective such as a high ability to respond to innovation and change and to local community and industry needs. College management was seen as particularly good at bringing in external finance. Staff student ratios, public relations image and classroom teaching were also though to be particularly efficient and effective but in contrast one person pointed out that

"the College is pre-occupied with external bodies rather than with job satisfaction inside."

Responses to the question on quality of work all related to the value and variety of the student experience, but a number of people mentioned other issues such as ensuring access to everyone in the community, the importance of job satisfaction to all college staff and the efficient use of resources. It was felt that the quality of work would be improved by a better relationship between management and staff and a stronger ethos of corporate identity and belonging. It was thought that quality of work would be improved by the acquisition of more staff and resources to fulfil more demands, and staff development and resources for the new F.E. While Quality Circles were considered to be capable of contributing to this process no examples were given of how this would occur and circles didn't feature in any comments that were made.

There was general agreement on a wide definition of curriculum, that it related to the total experience of students at the college, not just the requirements of the syllabus and that curriculum issues could include any point concerned with curriculum as defined in this way such as decoration of rooms. Few respondents wanted greater involvement in the curriculum although one person felt that greater information on curriculum changes at an earlier stage would be helpful. Level of involvement in curriculum issues varied with the position of staff in the organisation with support staff feeling relatively uninvolved and the Head of Department feeling very much involved. It was felt that curriculum decisions were made at too high a level and quality circles would be a useful way of influencing these decisions by making staff views known to management. Attention was drawn to the work of the Business Studies Circle which was felt to be particularly useful in solving curriculum problems.

General comments about the Quality Circle programme were pessimistic. One person felt that it had lost its way, was too reliant on support staff and was, therefore, peripheral to the main activities of the college. Unless teaching staff became more involved the programme wouldn't survive. Another stated that their main objection to Quality Circles was having to close down a department for two hours a week. One respondent saw Quality Circles being too serious when they should be fun.

Quality Circle Participants Questionnaire responses

Quality Circle participants saw similar problems with communications as other groups, with communications between sites being the worst aspect of the problem. Comments were made about feedback to staff from the Academic Board being variable and on the problems caused by departments all working differently.

Two comments seemed particularly heartfelt:

"We try to communicate but no-one seems to want to know"

"The place operates in a rush with no planning"

There was optimism about both the present and future ability of Quality Circles to improve matters but some scepticism about what would happen if the facilitator was changed in view of the cynical attitude of a majority of staff.

It was thought that Heads of Department worked well as a team but that others had difficulty in doing so. Quality Circles were seen to have improved communications which had led to better relationships, particularly between people working on different sites. Without a change in middle management attitudes however, there wasn't the scope for this to develop much further.

A majority of Quality Circle participants felt just about involved in the running of the College, but didn't really have much say and felt that people 'opted out' if there was too much unplanned change. While it was felt that Quality Circles could lead to greater involvement there was no evidence of this happening now or being likely to happen in the future.

The view of Quality Circle participants about efficiency and effectiveness in the College was that it was variable with problems including duplicated effort. It was felt that curriculum innovation was changing matters for the worse since staff were not given enough time to cope with the changes. Particularly efficient and effective aspects of college life were seen as the Quality Circle project on Insurance, classroom teaching, and the performance of the Principal and the Unions. Again Quality Circles were thought capable of influencing efficiency and effectiveness both now and in the future without any clear evidence of how this would happen.

Quality of work in the college context was seen as providing the services the public wants and needs, realising student potential, and promoting staff involvement and job satisfaction. Quality Circles were seen to have a role in improving the quality of work together with improved training opportunities.

There were mixed views about curriculum and curriculum issues reflecting the fact that most Quality Circle participants interviewed were members of the support staff. It was seen to be the teaching programme or the programme of courses delivered to the community. There was a view that it meant little to support staff since it was 'not deemed necessary for us to know'. In spite of this a number of respondents indicated that they had become interested in curriculum as a result of Quality Circle activity and wanted to know what was happening, particularly regarding new developments.

General views on Quality Circles were that the techniques could be much more widely used in meetings and that they helped personal development, but that members expected far too much of Quality Circle leaders.

COMMENTARY BY THE CONSULTANT

This was written following the interviews with opinion formers and Quality Circle participants during which the questionnaires were completed. Of the 20 staff interviewed 10 had been directly involved in quality circle activities and 10 had either no involvement or only slight involvement.

Those directly involved in Quality Circle activities
Achievements/Benefits:

The programme has been seen to provide a mechanism for bringing staff together (frequently for the first time) to discuss problems, resources and curriculum issues. Relatively few specific outcomes were reported but they included:

-Spring clean initiated by the office circle

-Sharpened administration by the library to reduce numbers of overdue books

-The success of the technicians presentation on Insurance

-The Chief Caretaker giving a talk to a circle

-The Principal writing to County Hall on Insurance.

Much more comment was made on less quantifiable benefits and improved communication was much to the fore. Linked to this was a strong and increased sense of feeling a part of the college and to some extent being involved in the decision making process. This, in turn, led to an appreciation and understanding of how decisions were made and, to a recognition that the problems of management were not as easily solved as people previously thought.

The experience of being trained and holding meetings produced a range of benefits. These included greater confidence in peoples' own abilities and a realisation that 'things can be changed'. The techniques were seen as valuable. They enabled open and frank discussion and prevented people making unjustified assumptions. Ideas were no longer allowed to 'float away into the atmosphere and be lost'. At a deeper level one quality circle leader claimed that the experience enabled him to put some theory into practice and in doing so to gain personal insights into his own behaviour. Overall, participation in circles was enjoyable, full of learning and had changed people's perceptions of college management in a positive way.

Obstacles/Constraints

Views expressed fell into two categories, some relatively neutral, followed by some strongly subjective comment. Finding time to meet was the most common difficulty and it was developed to include the problems presented by people's timetables and finding cover for classes. For support staff the practice of closing the office or the library for an hour a week was seen to present difficulties for other people. Closely related to time was the problem of split sites but a separate problem mentioned by some was the difficulty of finding a room in which the circle could meet.

A major hurdle mentioned by many was the widespread cynicism and antipathy displayed by staff not directly involved. One circle leader was 'appalled by the hostility shown to his circle'. On exploring this in more depth explanations offered included the assumption that people attending circle meetings were not working. It was also felt that there was apathy towards new initiatives, partly explained by the proliferation of them. In addition it was difficult to convince others of the benefits of becoming involved since there were as yet no major success stories.

Management Support

People's responses on this were rather variable. The overall conclusion was that there was room for improvement. Some of the comments were as follows:

"There is strong verbal support at the top, but I'm not sure if it will be put into action"

"If senior managers became involved this would be a role model for other managers"

"At middle management level it's not good - my boss is against Quality Circles"

"My own Head of Department is very supportive"

Future Developments

Those interviewed showed a small majority of optimism over pessimism. There was a strong feeling that an important problem would have to be tackled and solved so that those not yet involved would be encouraged to take part. It was also felt that the crucial role of facilitator should continue to be filled by someone as committed and able as the current post holder. Another view was that the whole process needed to be speeded up - *'70% done quickly would be far better than 100% done over a long time'*.

Those not directly involved in QC activities
Achievements/Benefits

Views expressed by this group, in the main, reflected those of the QC participants and there was little mention of specific outcomes. Those items mentioned were the spring clean and overdue books in the library. Much was made by this group of less tangible benefits they had observed. These included Quality Circles being the first opportunity many people have had to put their views forward in a constructive and ordered way and in so doing to feel more involved in college affairs. The programme had been seen to improve understanding of the working of the Academic Board and in general to aid staff in recognising that many of the problems facing the college were not easily solved.

Another perspective was the value of the Quality Circle 'code of conduct' and how this could help weaker members of a team in making their contribution. Overall Quality Circles were seen as providing an added dimension to staff development. However, two members of this group reported that Quality Circles had made no contact or impact on them. There was a single view that the benefits had been only marginal and were nothing which could not have been achieved by staff meeting more frequently.

Obstacles/Constraints

Similar comments were made to those by the Quality Circle Members and included the difficulties associated with making time and people available. The 'disruptive' effect of closing departments received somewhat more comment than from the other group. It was also felt that the organisational structure of the college was not conducive to Quality Circle operations. On the matter of people's attitudes towards Quality Circles, this group repeated points made by the Quality Circle members on scepticism, cynicism and suspicion. They also broadened the point to indicate that Quality Circles were not yet seen as a broadly acceptable cross college activity which had entered the culture and become a topic of everyday conversation. A majority held the view that the money spent on the programme had caused these negative perceptions.

A major additional contribution by this group on constraints to Quality Circle development was a set of perceptions of the proliferation and lack of effectiveness of other meetings and committees. This point was one of the stronger matters arising during the evaluation. Typical comments were:

"We've got meeting mania"

"There is a failure of our committees to come up with results"

"Due to there being committees for everything, Quality Circles are relegated to trivial matters"

One view put forward on the general matter of constraints on Quality Circles was the initial suspicion on the part of NATFHE but it was felt that this was no longer the case.

Management Support

As before, people saw this in varying ways. Overall, the negative and positive comments were in balance. One Head of Department spoke of his personal learning from having a circle in the department; another felt "detached" from circles.

Future Developments

This group were slightly more evenly balanced between optimism and pessimism than the Quality Circle members. There were two major concerns. One being the lack of a major contribution from teaching staff in the programme. The other was a genuinely felt doubt about the relevance of Quality Circles in education. Clearly there is a measure of interdependence between these concerns and as yet there is insufficient evidence to judge which, if any, is pre-eminent.

EFFECTS OF QUALITY CIRCLES ON ORGANISATIONAL CULTURE

Quality Circles are an Organisational Development tool employed with the objective of changing organisational culture. At Accrington and Rossendale College they have helped to crystallise some of the inherent problems faced by F.E. staff as they struggle to come to terms with outside pressures to become more efficient and effective via modern management styles and methods. It can be seen from the questionnaire responses that broadly speaking Senior Management, Heads of Department and Senior Lecturers, all who have some degree of management responsibility have been supportive of the experiment as have support staff who have seen Quality Circles as the first opportunity they have ever had to express their views. However the largest single group of staff in the College, the Lecturers were cynical from the start, and if anything had their cynicism confirmed during the period of the project. Some time after the completion of the project a seminar was held with a group of Lecturers to explore the reasons for this.

It became clear that the initial Quality Circle presentations had made many Lecturers realise that there was a management structure in the College they had been aware of without realising its significance. Many had taken the view that since in education the staff are "professionals" everyone was part of the same structure but simply fulfilling different functions. They saw the real management as being outside the College at LEA level. Traditionally those staff in senior positions inside the College were seen as their natural allies freeing them to concentrate on what they saw as their real task, the teaching/learning process. Now they had confirmed for them via Quality Circles what they had felt for some time that management posts inside the College were the high status posts with the post holders privy to all manner of "secret information" which the lecturing staff could only guess at. This was clearly a threat to the status of the lecturing staff and in the face of this threat their first instinct was to take refuge in what they saw as the fundamental core of the job, *their* students, and *their* subject, and as professional presenters of information snipe at the way in which Quality Circles had been introduced which was described as being "amateurish" and from a management point of view. It was apparent that once the fear of change was established Lecturers were prepared to take every opportunity to be critical and in many ways Quality Circles provided a scapegoat for other things staff were unhappy about such as staff promotions for management tasks rather than teaching ability.

Against this background Quality Circles were seen as a management "trick" a way of finding staff to promote who would effectively be management pawns. At the time they were introduced morale was so low that they couldn't possibly succeed. Lecturers felt they had enough problems of their own with curriculum changes and coping with a wider range of students without being called upon to solve management problems too when others would only claim the credit for all their hard work! It had been wrong to introduce Quality Circles as a means of solving management problems, Lecturers would have responded much better to the presentation of problems as "our problems" or the "Colleges' problems". Quality Circles were seen as too much of a "top down exercise". More should have been done to build the experiment from the grass roots.

Quality Circles could be seen to have had quite a strong impact on College culture by helping to bring home to staff a number of changed realities and in the process changing staff perceptions about their role, the role of the College and the role of College management. However, although Quality Circles offer a means of staff being involved in and coming to terms with change, in our case they tended to lead to a hardening of attitudes, and defence of entrenched positions amongst many lecturing staff.

THE FUTURE OF QUALITY CIRCLES IN THE COLLEGE

The Quality Circle programme is suffering from many of the problems which have affected the American programmes. In Bartlett's (1983) terms it is surviving but certainly not flourishing. In spite of the care taken over the introduction of the programme the problem of cynicism amongst teaching staff has never been overcome. All agree that Quality Circles can have a role and can be useful but most are unprepared to commit themselves to the programme given their workload and the lack of confidence in existing structures which are seen to pay lip service only to the notion of consultation. The questionnaire responses indicate clearly the range of problems which different sectors of staff have, many of which would lend themselves to Quality Circle approaches. However the commitment isn't there and the level of distrust of the consultant and of senior management increases as one moves down the hierarchy with the exception of support staff who have been committed to the concept from the start and have shown great loyalty to the consultant in particular. Quality Circles have been equated with a business approach which hasn't been helpful. With hindsight, during the early presentations to all staff and during the early training events the use of examples from the American educational experience of Quality Circles rather than manufacturing examples would have been helpful. The views of Dore (1983) and of Bradley and Hill (1983) are borne out in that the levels of trust necessary for a successful Quality Circle programme simply aren't there at present.

One of the problems in promoting circles amongst teaching staff has been in defining the 'natural work group'. It is interesting that the three most successful Quality Circles have been in the clearly defined areas of library staff, technician staff, and administrative staff. Staff in these groups have identified closely with each other and with the problems they face. Undoubtedly had teaching staff been organised into sectional or departmental workrooms more Quality Circles would have formed, and in fact the one circle which did form solely amongst teaching staff included a number of staff based in one workroom. It is clear from the questionnaire responses that Quality Circles are associated with peripheral issues, and are seen as being almost exclusively concerned with support staff. Because of this the programme now has an 'image problem' to overcome if it is to develop amongst teaching staff. However honest the intentions of Senior Management have been in introducing Quality Circles the necessary changes in management style shown to be vital in Schafer's (1983) experience of Quality Circles in an American Community College simply haven't taken place. A much more interpersonal style of management needs to be widespread in the College to nurture a development as democratic as Quality Circles. The fact is reflected in the perception of teaching staff, many of whom were suspicious of senior management at the start. Where their suspicions were confirmed and reinforced by middle management views and actions the incentive to join Quality Circles disappeared. As far as the Circles which do exist are concerned it is doubtful just how long people at a fairly low level in the hierarchy can maintain enthusiasm when they feel there is hostility around them and the situation isn't improving.

A number of staff have claimed that they simply didn't know about the Quality Circle programme, but the programme has had a high profile. There were presentations to all staff at the start, the consultant has directly interviewed around 10% of staff and at least 25% of staff have received questionnaires. All progress and achievements have been publicised. No opportunities to write about the programme in the College weekly staff bulletin have been missed. Quality Circles have been featured in the College newsletter for industry and commerce and the programme has featured in a local radio broadcast. Updating seminars have also been held for staff. Some must spend so much time in their ivory towers that they are simply unaware of what is going on around them.

Quality Circles are suffering from a lack of resources, often at a very basic level such as no rooms being available for meetings which has led, on occasions, to 10 people being crammed into a small office for a Quality Circle meeting. The problem of recognition of circle achievements has never been adequately solved. Circle leaders and members have claimed that a successful presentation is recognition enough but this seems doubtful. An ideal form of recognition would have been the provision of a room for Quality Circle meetings but this did not prove possible.

It has proved relatively straighforward during the period of the project to provide cover for administrative and clerical staff attending Circle meetings but the decision, once the programme was established, not to give any remission from teaching duties to teaching staff on the basis that Quality Circles should not take precedence over any other form of staff development activity proved a major disincentive fuelling the belief that management wanted something for nothing. Early in the programme when training did benefit from remission they were well supported.

The consultant's view and the indication from other programmes is that for four fully functioning circles and an expanding programme at least a half time facilitator is required but there has been an unwillingness to commit this level of staff time to the project. Priorities are always difficult but Quality Circles have involved between 10% and 15% of staff on a regular basis and have generated a great deal of goodwill amongst those involved with potentially massive spin offs for the organisation. This should have been taken into account.

In the later stages of the project Union action relating to a national pay claim proved a problem preventing the provision of training courses for those staff who had declared an interest in their questionnaire responses. This would have led to an expansion of the programme with consequent boost to morale. There is evidence too that the work of the Business Studies Circle, favourably commented on by HMI is becoming more widely appreciated in the College which might bode well for the future of circles amongst teaching staff.

The Academic Board's decisions to distance itself from the Quality Circle programme at an early stage was not helpful since the Academic Board is the primary formal channel for staff views to be represented. A reporting process through the co-ordinating committee to the Academic Board would have been useful in publicising Quality Circle activity and in linking it to the formal structure of College organisation.

There have been many positive aspects to the programme. The staff development opportunity offered to support staff, long neglected in terms of training, was welcomed and has led to support staff representation on the Academic Board Staff Development Sub Committee. Support staff involvement on in-house training courses, such as computing courses is now common and they are now likely to include the full range of staff from Heads of Department to clerical assistants. Support staff have become aware of their potential through Quality Circles and their growth in confidence has been immense. An onlooker would be unable to distinguish between teaching and support staff at a circle meeting where a technician or clerk/typist might be handling a brainstorming session with great skill. The comment was made by one technician that -

"I've worked here for 20 years and this is the first time I've been asked for my opinion and felt I could contribute."

One lesson of the quality circle programme is the revelation of a massive under-utilisation of support staff given their real abilities.

The Business Studies circle has certainly experienced some of the benefits that Field and Harrison (1983) found (see Page), particularly the one relating to the need for curriculum decisions to be taken by those who are going to implement them. Since the questionnaire responses revealed a view that curriculum decisions are made at too high a level in the College this could be a way to promote further Quality Circles amongst teaching staff. However, one of the basic problems for a Quality Circle is to come to terms with its own power to change things. Management can no longer be blamed to the same extent!

Quality Circles have, of course, actually solved problems, many of which were causing great difficulty to those experiencing them but which College management were unaware of. They have been shown to be valuable in avoiding rushed decisions and the use of the techniques in other settings has proved valuable as a team building exercise for example when working parties or committees have met for the first time. One potentially very useful activity has been the drawing up of guidelines for conducting College meetings produced during a quality circles training event.

Inadequate support at all management levels, lack of resources, cynical attitudes and low morale amongst some staff all indicate that over a period of time the quality circles programme will struggle and although one or two circles will continue owing to the enthusiasm of the leaders these too might eventually suffer from the fatigue factor. This is not a disaster. A great deal has been learned along the way and there are many positive achievements. The experience parallels exactly what has happened to most of the quality circle programmes in American educational institutions, neither have the programmes at High Peak College and Barnfield College Luton flourished once the initial impetus was removed. However, this is not an indictment of quality circles which do have massive potential, if the will is there and the framework is right.

In the long term if Quality Circles are to succeed at Accrington and Rossendale College a great deal of work needs to be done to develop an atmosphere of constructive change in which all staff can play a part. There are many OD approaches which could be tried. A first step could be the involvement of senior staff in leading seminars for all staff in small groups discussing current issues affecting the College and the responses that are being made, explaining management views and the reasons for decisions. Teaching staff could all be involved in quality circle related activity by the use of the techniques in other contexts, first of all demonstrated by senior staff in the conduct of routine meetings and then used by others. The guidelines already exist for doing this and it would demonstrate a clear commitment by all management to quality circles. Perhaps since one of the problems for Quality Circles has been slow progress, these vergroups should work to short term targets which would give clear evidence of success. More awareness of group dynamics should be built into training for members of quality circle related groups to help ensure they are involved and less reliant on the leader.

Finally, in order to maintain interest and keep a quality circle programme fresh it might be beneficial to abandon the idea of quality circles which are almost perpetual as the membership changes in favour of an annual programme which ends each June and starts from scratch in September. Meanwhile the College does have an active programme of four circles, a committed facilitator, and a backlog of staff awaiting training opportunities. It may yet take off.

THE IMPLICATIONS OF INTRODUCING A QUALITY CIRCLESPROGRAMME FOR OTHER COLLEGES

The most important aspect of introducing a Quality Circles programme is to accurately assess management style in the institution concerned and staff perceptions of that management style (see fig. 3) Opportunities only exist for Quality Circles in an organisation where managers are perceived as colleagues rather than bosses and where genuine delegation of authority and responsibility

Figure 3

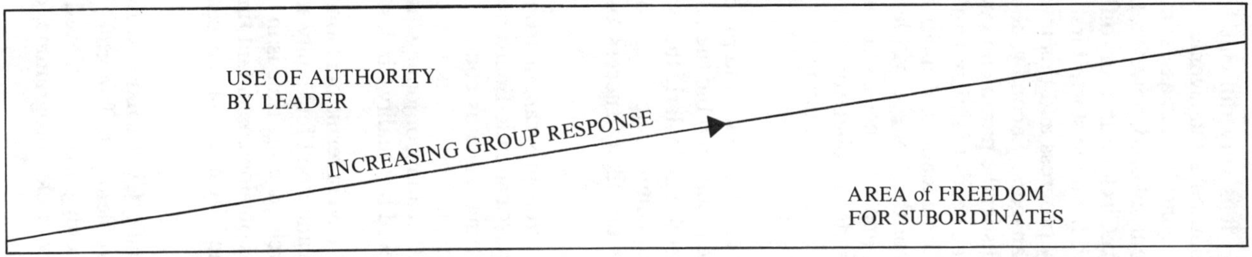

```
              USE OF AUTHORITY
                 BY LEADER
                              ──────────►
                      INCREASING GROUP RESPONSE

                                              AREA of FREEDOM
                                              FOR SUBORDINATES
```

Management Style	TELLS	SELLS	CONSULTS	DELEGATES	SHARES
Leaders Behaviour	PLANS; DIRECTS; DECIDES.		PLANS; STEERS SEEKS VIEWS.	COORDINATES; SHARES CONTROL	
Group Behaviour	Accepts orders; has no influence on decisions.	Accepts orders with reasons; only passive influences on decisions.	Gives own viewpoint: makes requests and complaints influences opinions.	Accepts responsibility for action and achievements.	Contributes with full potential; leadership may rotate among members.
Opportunities for Quality Circles	None	A Few	Many, with careful introduction.	Many	Full, but may have a system not requiring

takes place leading to the development of trust. It is very difficult for an organisation to take an objective view of its position on a management style continuum and it is therefore important to involve a consultant in assessing this before Quality Circles are mentioned. It must be remembered, however, that a consultant coming into a College to introduce Quality Circles is in a very difficult position and a number of issues need to be clarified from the start. Firstly, he must be clear that the management style will allow progress and this involves talking to a cross-section of staff, not just senior managers. Secondly, he must be clear what is expected of him and that this is realistic; the parameters within which he can operate must be made clear. Thirdly, he needs to satisfy a number of people, possibly with conflicting objectives e.g. Circle leaders, Principal, the funding body. A failure to understand the ethos of the College will lead to difficulties. In our case the consultant trod the fine line with success in spite of the resistance he met from teaching staff. A matrix style of College organisation may well benefit the development of a quality circle programme if it has genuinely led to fewer blocks to cross college developments.

All staff need to be carefully introduced to Quality Circle theory and practice. The industrial and commercial successes need to be mentioned but the educational experience and possibilities need to be stressed, particularly the way in which Quality Circles could be used to consider curriculum issues. Responses to this initial introduction is a clear indicator of the likely success of the programme.

It is important to gain a wide acceptance of a quality circle programme from the formal structures in the organisation particularly the Academic Board and to promote a discussion of quality circles in other settings such as course team meetings, ensuring that the voluntary nature of quality circles is not compromised in any way by either intimidating people into leading or joining quality circles or intervening in the choice of topics considered by Quality Circles.

It is vital to ensure that quality circles are fully supported in terms of resources. In particular that staff have time to attend meetings and don't feel guilty about this taking them away from other work. Quality Circle meeting time is in itself very productive work. Adequate facilitator time and outside consultant time is also important. All participants in quality circle activity must have access to adequate training.

Any organisation considering the introduction of Quality Circles must be aware of the potential benefits in terms of solution of problems, staff morale, and improved ways of working in teams. These may be only partially achieved but there are no disadvantages to establishing a quality circles programme, only varied levels of success.

THE EXTENT TO WHICH THE ORIGINAL PROJECT AIMS HAVE BEEN ACHIEVED

In terms of the four aims listed in the original project proposal staff have clearly been involved in participatory management through quality circle activity. Management related problems have been considered and decisions made which have been accepted by management. The process has been largely confined to support staff although with the help of teaching staff. The evidence is that the one quality circle composed entirely of teaching staff is likely to make recommendations which are a distinct challenge to management views and may lead to changes in management policy. A model for introducing quality circles into a College has been established and is clearly transferable to other Colleges. Lessons have been learned in terms of refining the model for more effective use in the educational context. Some measure of the effectiveness of the model has been achieved by the questionnaire, based on anticipated benefits of quality circles, administered to various groups of staff and although the results of this questionnaire are highly subjective they do give an indication of the impact of quality circles on the College. The staff development implications are evident from the way the opportunity has ben seized by support staff in particular. Everyone involved has undergone training in all the basic techniques and has benefited from both the acquisition of these skills and the confidence in their new found abilities. The questionnaire responses reveal an attitude shift across the College about what can be achieved through quality circles and although this is probably minimal at present in the case of most teaching staff this could well change as the techniques are used more widely.

In terms of the five expectations detailed by the Principal, Quality Circles have undoubtedly provided the means to involve more staff in the management of the College. The questionnaire responses provide clear feedback on this revealing that some staff felt that although not enough was being made of existing opportunities current management systems needed improving before others were introduced. Heads of Department felt that power delegated to Quality Circles would produce results but did equate quality circles with administrative and organisational management rather than management of the curriculum. Some staff were even sceptical over whether management would implement quality circle solutions to problems, and although there was a wish for more 'people centred' management there was a view that Quality Circles hadn't contributed to this. Lecturers, although considering that curriculum decisions were taken at too high a level didn't see quality circles as a means of influencing this process. All of these views together with the feelings of resentment and manipulation referred to, caused by the introduction of quality circles are evidence of some confusion and a lack of preparedness for a quality circle programme. It is interesting that even though quality circle participants have clearly been involved in management decisions they don't perceive this as having been the case.

In the course of the programme there has been much evidence that 'the quality of what people say is not connected with their status in the College' and that 'everyone has a right to be heard' since for the first time support staff have been given a channel to present views direct to the Principal and the quality of the presentations made has fully justified his belief in Quality Circles.

The third of the Principal's expectations was that Quality Circles would clarify lines of communication both inside the College and outside and the questionnaire responses show that all staff have been aware of the difficulties of internal communications caused by the split site nature of the College. All groups except lecturers and senior lecturers felt that Quality Circles had significantly contributed to improved communications. The consultant's commentary on the interviews he conducted indicates that Quality Circles have made staff more aware of management difficulties but as far as 'lines of communication' are concerned there is always a danger that Quality Circles because they operate outside the formal structure will contribute to confusion such as when they and other groups are working on different aspects of the same problem. The facilitator needs sensitive antennae to pick up all of these possible implications of Quality Circle activity and to ensure that the overlaps are constructive. As far as external communications are concerned all Quality Circles making presentations have been made very aware of the County Hall dimension in College decision making and the difficulties this can cause.

In terms of the College benefiting from a more participative approach this is only likely to be the case if most people are participating and since the total number of people involved in Quality Circles has been relatively low (around 10% - 15% of staff) and that there has been some hostility from other staff it is doubtful whether Quality Circles have brought about a greater cohesion. However, those who have been involved have benefited and the College has benefited from the work.

The final point of the Principal's expectations related to the usefulness of Quality Circle skills and techniques in other areas of college work and this transference has certainly occurred and proved beneficial, both through the code of conduct for meetings and the use of the techniques for team building. At least one department is using Quality Circle techniques as a feature of staff meetings to determine departmental priorities.

The long list of benefits anticipated by opinion formers [see page 45] at the start of the project have all been achieved to a greater or lesser extent as revealed in the questionnaire analysis. If one goes down the list examples could be given against each of the points made although these would not be of major significance in some instances. The final element of evaluation is the continuation of a

Quality Circle programme beyond the life of the project, and it is continuing despite the difficulties through a core of highly involved and committed staff.

EVALUATING QUALITY CIRCLES IN A COLLEGE OF FURTHER EDUCATION

SUMMARY

Definition Quality Circles are small volunteer groups of workers who meet for an hour a week with a trained leader operating to a strict code of conduct and use techniques of brainstorming, cause and effect classification, pareto analysis and presentation to consider work related problems and recommend solutions to management which are then implemented unless there are very good reasons for not doing so.

Background

Quality Circles are based on Western ideas but developed first in Japan before spreading throughout the world. They could be considered to be in the mainstream of the human relations movement in industrial relations and can be a valuable tool when used by consultants and other practitioners involved in organisation development. Around 300 firms in the U.K. have introduced Quality Circles and the main benefits have been found to be enhanced employee motivation and involvement, and cost effectiveness. Quality Circles have been tried in educational institutions in North America but there have been only two Quality Circle related experiments in the U.K. both of which bear distinct differences from the pure Quality Circles model.

Most research and publicity about Quality Circles has been supportive of the concept but some writers have argued that organisational culture in the West is so different from Japan that Quality Circles can't succeed in the long term. It is often argued that education is different, but there are many parallels between Colleges and the service sector of industry such as intangible problems, a workforce spread between sites making meetings difficult, and Quality Circles not being close enough to the systems they want to change.

In North American educational institutions Quality Circles have been used to tackle a wide range of problems, mainly amongst support staff. They have been generally unsuccessful because of the absence of participatory management styles, lack of commitment from all levels of management, the proliferation of committees, inadequate resources and lack of a clear definition of Quality Control. However, many individuals have benefited from increased job satisfaction, participation, 'ownership' of solutions and greater efficiency.

Quality Circles at Accrington and Rossendale College

Accrington and Rossendale College is a medium sized College working on eight major sites and like similar institutions is suffering problems of low morale in a period of rapid change. The management structure has remained relatively traditional and Quality Circles offered an opportunity to develop participation alongside existing structures. Further Education Unit funding enabled the College to use an established management consultant and operate a Quality Circle programme as a research project. Project aims were agreed as follows:

-To involve staff in participatory management

-To evolve and test a Quality Circle model which is transferable to other institutions

-To evaluate the effectiveness of the model

-To evaluate Quality Circles as a process of staff development.

The programme was carefully introduced to staff at a series of meetings and their views were canvassed. The Academic Board which represents staff views was consulted. The Principal made clear his support for the project and volunteers were sought to undergo leader training. Following the training, four Circles formed, one amongst library staff, one amongst technician staff (but led by a member of the teaching staff), one amongst administrative staff (which included members of the teaching staff) and one amongst teaching staff in the Business and Management Studies Department, involving in total 10 - 15% of college staff. Problems considered have included overdue library books, the operation of BTEC Courses, insurance, the external appearance of the College and storage space. Three of the Circles have made presentations to management. The programme has been managed by a project Steering Committee, a Project Director operating as Quality Circle facilitator, and a Co-ordinating Committee consisting of the Principal, Quality Circle leaders, Union representatives, facilitator and representatives of various College functions. This group, in addition to advising and supporting circle leaders and constantly reviewing progress has helped to organise training for Quality Circle members, trainers, and middle managers. The professional expertise and experience of the Consultant has been invaluable throughout.

Evaluation

Evaluation has been on the basis of progress and problems as the project has progressed, the benefits expected by key staff at the start of the project and the extent to which the Principal's aims have been met and the FEU aims achieved. A questionnaire was devised and distributed to one in five staff. The questionnaire was also the basis for face to face interviews with key staff, and Quality Circle participants. Questions concentrated on attitudes to communications, team work, sense of involvement, efficiency and effectiveness, quality of work, curriculum and curriculum issues and the effects of the Quality Circle programme on all of these.

Results.

There have been many benefits resulting from the Quality Circle programme. Particularly important has been the staff development opportunity offered to support staff, long neglected in terms of training. They have become aware of their potential, their contribution to the curriculum, and as their confidence grows they are making demands. An onlooker would be unable to distinguish between teaching and support staff at a circle where a technician or clerk/typist might be handling a brainstorming session with great skills. Circles have led to the actual solution of problems which were causing great difficulty to those actually experiencing them even though College Management were unaware.

Quality Circles have proved of great value in avoiding rushed decision making showing that the most obvious solution is often not the best one, and that all options must be considered. The techniques themselves have been particularly helpful in other settings such as Course team meetings, College Working Parties, Academic Board Sub-Committees, and as a device for team building. There is a consensus that Circles have a role to play in most aspects of College life.

As might be expected there have also been a number of problems associated with quality circles. There has been some opposition from middle managers who have failed to see quality circles as "real work" and have discouraged staff from attending meetings. The main opposition however has come from Lecturing staff some of whom, in a climate of change in F.E. have seen circles as one change too many, exemplified by the comments

"Management are paid to manage, why should we do it for them?"

and

"What is the Principal up to now?".

The existence of a circle programme inevitably creates a new power base that demands consideration and existing management structures may in the long term prove too autocratic and unsupportive to ensure the survival of the quality circle programme. Quality Circle techniques while proving very effective for solving administrative, organisational, and technical problems may be too inflexible to solve Central Curriculum problems. Finally Circles can take a long time to achieve results and the problems they choose to work on can seem peripheral to everyone except the circle members themselves.

Introducing Quality Circles to a College

The lessons learned very much reflect earlier research in the industrial and commercial context and also the North American Educational experience. For Circles to succeed in any organisation the management style should be as open and participative as possible, the programme must be thoroughly supported and encouraged at all levels of management, many of the blocks to Circle success are at middle management level. A climate of trust must be developed. When the concept is introduced to teaching staff they will be happier if educational precedents are stressed. Examples from industry and commerce may provoke a cynical reaction. Circles undoubtedly work best amongst 'natural work groups' such as humanities staff, or history staff, they are particularly valuable, and perhaps most effective amongst support staff. Circles must be given adequate resources such as consultant time, facilitator time, places to meet, remission from teaching duties. They also need the support of the formal structure of the organisation such as the Academic Board.

Quality Circles are not a panacea, but they can have dramatic results in terms of staff involvement, morale, and identification with the aims of the organisation. There are no disadvantages to introducing a Quality Circle programme only varied levels of success.

Bibliography

Argyris C. 1957 Personality and Organisation New York, Harper & Bros.

Argyris C. 1970 Intervention Theory and Method. A Behavioural Science View London, Addison Wesley.

Bandy B. 1984 Quality Circles in State Government and Education Cincinnati, I.A.Q.C. Press.

Bartlett J. 1983 Success and Failure in Quality Circles. A Study of 25 Companies Sheffield M.S.C.

Bernstein B. 1971 Class Codes and Control. Theoretical Studies towards a Sociology of Language Vol.1 London, Routledge and Kegan Paul.

Blacker G. 12/3/87 'Keeping Town Hall Staff on their Toes' in The Times London.

Blundell C. April 1986, 'Quality Circles Bottom Up Staff Development. An Organic Process. Progress Report' in Association of Professional Tutors Journal Vol.1, No.2, pages 7-17.

Bradley K. and Hill S. November 1983 'After Japan : The Quality Circle Transplant and Productive Efficiency' in British Journal of Industrial Relations Vol.XXI, No.3, pages 291-308.

Christenson G. (Editor) May, 1986 Quality Circles Network in Education Newsletter Oklahoma State University.

Dale B. and Lees J. December 1986 Quality Circle Programme Development some key issues Sheffield M.S.C.

Department of Trade and Industry June 1985 Quality Circles London.

Dore R. 1983 Introduction to Japan in the Passing Lane by Satoshi Kamuta, London, Allen and Unwin.

Drucker 1979 Management London Pan Books.

Faux R. 20/1/87 'Management in the Round' in The Times London.

Felton D. 19/1/87 'Job of going around in Quality Circles' in The Independent London.

FEU 1984 Policy Statement, Staff Development for Support Staff in Further Education London.

FEU Conference Report 1986 'A Neglected Issue' Staff Development for Support Staff London.

FEU 1987 Curriculum Led Institutional Development London.

FEU 1987 The College Does it Better London.

Field M.J. and Harrison A.B. March 1983, 'Quality Circles. A Strategy for Personal and Curriculum Development Coombe Lodge Working paper 1803

Gammie A. 16/2/86 'Company Employee Interest' in The Times London

Galbraith M. and Christian G. March 1986 'A Quality Circle implementation process for Higher Education' in Quality Circle Journal Vol.9, pages 10-14.

French W. and Bell C. 1978 Organisation Development, Behavioural Science Intervention for Organisation improvement Englewood Cliffs N.J., Prentice Hall.

Harrison R. 1975 'Diagnosing Organisation Ideology' Annual Handbook for Group Facilitators pages 101-105.

Harrison R. 1975 'Understanding Your Organisation's Character' Annual Handbook for Group Facilitators pages 199-209.

Herzberg F. 1968 Work and the Nature of Man London, Crosby Lockwood Staples.

Ingle S. 1982 Quality Circles Master Guide Englewood Cliffs N.J., Prentice Hall.

Ishikawa K. 1972 Japan Quality Control Tokyo: Juse.

Kay C. and Buch K. 1986 Do Quality Circles make a difference? A study of Quality Circles at Iowa State University. Ames, Iowa State University Press.

Keefe J. and Gibson P. August 1981 'Point Part-Time Facilitation Counter Point Full-Time Facilitation' in Quality Circles Journal Vol.IV, pages 8-9.

Lane J. October 1983 'Management Techniques in Education Administration' in School Business Affairs Vol.49, Part 10, pages 34-38.

Lawson K. and Tubbs L. Spring 1986 'Quality Circles an experiment in Higher Education' in NASPA Journal pages 35-45.

Lynn Moretz H. 1983 'Teampower and Brainwork' Quality Circles at Central Piedmont Community College Q.C. Sources : Selected writings on Quality Circles IAQC Press, pages 297-308.

Maslow A. 1970 Motivation and Personality New York, Harper and Row.

McGregor D. 1960 The Human Side of Enterprise Boston, McGraw-Hill.

McGregor D. 1966 Leadership and Motivation Boston, Massachusetts Institute of Technology Press.

Mullard December 1986, Quality Circles Newsletter, Circle News Issue No.17.

Nichol J.B. 1981 'The Team Development Process' in Management for Health Administration edited by Alan D.E. and Hughes J., Pitman.

O'Hare P. June 1986 Quality Circles in Further Education ISM Project, Accrington and Rossendale College.

Osborne O. 1986 'Quality Circles: The key to improving productivity in the Service Section' Paper given to the World Conference on Continuing Engineering Education.

Robson M. 1982 Quality Circles a Practical Guide Aldershot, Gower.

Robson M. 1984 Quality Circles in Action Aldershot, Gower.

Schafer E. 1983 Sharing Lane Community College's experience of Quality Circles Lane Community College.

Skibbens C. March 1986 'Can Quality Circles create solutions to the problems of American Public Education?' Quality Circles Journal Vol.9, pages 6-9.

Transport and General Workers Union 1984 Quality Circles Policy Statement

Appendix 1

IDEAS AD LIB' QUALITY CIRCLE

OVERDUE BOOKS

PRESENTATION TO MANAGEMENT

March 3rd 1987

Introduction

When the 'Ideas Ad Lib' Quality Circle was originally formed, it consisted of eleven members of the Library staff, representing each of the libraries on five sites. However, the Circle has now been reduced to four members. Possible reasons for the reduction in membership are:

1. There were practical problems involved in actually getting to hold meetings. For example, libraries had to be closed to allow so many people to attend; staff had to travel between sites, sometimes on public transport, to the meetings; several staff work part-time only and it was difficult to arrange a time when someone wasn't off duty.

2. With eleven members, the Circle seemed too large for people to feel comfortable and for the Circle to work effectively. It would appear that the optimum number for a Circle should be less than this number. In hindsight, with two leaders available, it may have been better to form two Circles, meeting at different times and working on separate problems.

3. Some of the staff, finding the concept of Quality Circle management outside their previous experience, seemed to regard the value of the system with a degree of scepticism.

4. From the point of view of the management in the library, it appeared that a large number of staff-hours were being spent on the project at the regular meetings, training sessions for leaders, etc. without the equivalent benefit to the library service being in evidence.

However, although the preceding comments may seem to be on the negative side regarding the value of Quality Circles, we shall later be looking at the benefits gained from the formation of this Circle.

The work of the Circle

After some initial basic training on the procedures of Quality Circle meetings by the two leaders, a brainstorming session was held to examine the problems encountered in the various libraries and more than twenty problems were put forward for consideration. After a vote was taken, it was decided by an overwhelming majority to tackle the problem of overdue books. This is a problem which all libraries face and to which there is seemingly no completely satisfactory solution. However, the problem can be reduced by positive action and thereby increase the efficiency and effectiveness of the library service.

The effects of overdue books on the library service

1. Books are not available on the shelves to other readers.

2. Staff time is needed to locate and reserve the book.

3. Staff time is needed to find alternative sources of information for the reader.

4. Costs are incurred if it is necessary to borrow books through the inter-library loan system.

5. The longer a book is on loan, the greater the likelihood of the book being lost.

6. Staff time and money are required to send out reminders for overdue books.

7. Further time and administrative costs are needed to invoice readers for lost books.

8. There is a loss of revenue when books are lost, as money received does not revert to the book fund.

9. The book fund is further depleted when there is a necessity to replace lost books.

10. In order to be cost effective, a book must be used as much as possible in order to gain the maximum usage for the cost of the book. Books kept overdue and unused are not good value for money.

11. The inability to fulfil readers' requirements quickly, reduces the effectiveness of the library service and affects attitudes towards the quality of the service provided.

A brainstorm on the causes of the problem, followed by a cause and effect analysis, highlighted the problems which were felt by the majority of the Circle to lie in our "methods" (see Annexe No.1).

Data Collection

The Circle then went on to gather statistics to indicate the size of the problem and a Pareto analysis showed that by far the largest number of overdue books were those borrowed by staff (see Annexe No.2).

One of the causes of this problem seemed to be that too many library tickets were issued to some members of staff, leading to a build-up of "private libraries".

Also staff overdue reminders have not been sent frequently enough in the past, although the frequency varied from one site to another. It was felt that this also gave rise to the possibility that staff would forget that they had ever borrowed a particular book, leading to lost book stock. The fact that the library does not charge fines leads to a lack of concern as to whether books are overdue or not. The Tutor Librarian investigated Lancashire County policy on this matter, and was informed by the Deputy County Librarian that it is not County policy to charge fines in College libraries. Quality Circle members in general were not in favour of a system of fines, which can be counter-productive, and would also be time consuming to administer.

The final incentive to students to return overdue books has, at all sites, been an invoice, sent after three ignored reminders. This invoice lists all the non-returned books with their replacement cost. Invoices have not been sent routinely to staff, their overdue items remaining on file almost indefinitely.

Beyond sending invoices we have no further action to take, beyond passing the outstanding invoices to the District Education Office, which results in those books being written off.

Discussion on these points raised the side issue of monies which are paid into County funds to compensate for lost books. This money does not, at present come back to the College library, to enable replacement books to be bought, resulting in a depletion of the library stock. The Chief Administrative Officer was consulted on this point, and he got in touch with the County Treasurer's Office. The official contacted said that he would be willing to arrange for the money to be re-directed to the library, although this was not County procedure, and he did not wish to be quoted. He felt that an approach from the College Principal could result in a change on this score.

It was felt generally that a standardisation and tightening up of procedure for issuing books and tickets to staff and students would lead to some improvement and reduce the numbers of overdue and missing library books.

A system of registration was considered, but rejected after discussion, as it was felt with the rapid turnover of student population, this was likely to prove difficult and time consuming.

Some of the procedures already taking place at the Rossendale site were taken on board by the other sites. In this way we have learnt from other libraries, who had previously attempted to tackle the problem and whose system seemed most appropriate. This included numbering the four tickets the students were allowed and date-stamping them on the reverse to prevent abuse of the system. No tickets were to be issued to students unless formal identification was provided to attempt to clamp down on the numbers of false addresses given to staff. It was decided to inform the students verbally of the changes to the system and also by a notice, standing on the library counter at each site and this has been found to be extremely useful in reducing extra work and repetition by the staff. (see Annexe No.3).

It was decided to inform staff of changes by means of a 'Bulletin' which we felt should be lighthearted and amusing in order to have some impact (see Annexe No.4). The Circle felt that the text must be given some sort of current theme and 'Christmas' was eventually decided upon.

After some deliberation and discussion, the Bulletin took the form of a 'Diary' based on the 'Adrian Mole' book and was distributed in mid-December to all members of staff. The 'Bulletin' covered the changes which were to take place:

> 1. Staff are now only allowed 10 tickets.
>
> 2. Length of loan standardised to 1 month at all sites.
>
> 3. An overdue reminder will be sent when books are initially one month overdue and thereafter once a month if books have not been returned (see Annexe No.5).
>
> 4. After three overdue reminders have been ignored an invoice is sent to both staff and students. Staff have previously rarely been invoiced and overdues only sent at th end of the academic year.

Benefits

We hoped to achieve benefits from these changes:

> 1. To make people more _aware_ of the need to return library books.
>
> 2. To attempt to change their _attitudes_ towards books and towards the library. This problem of _attitudes_ was found to be one of the major causes when we worked through Cause Classification and it was hoped that by tackling our _methods_ of running the system that a 'knock on' effect would be an improvement in their general attitude.
>
> 3. To make it less likely that books would be lost, which produces a financial benefit when books do not have to be replaced.
>
> 4. To ensure that more books are always available and on the shelves.
>
> 5. To benefit staff, students and the library service as a whole by the standardisation of procedures across sites, avoiding annoyance and confusion at irregularities and also improving efficiency.

We must say that as this is an on-going project it will be difficult to see the full benefits until the end of the year. However, we have produced an intermediate pareto analysis to compare with the previous statistics. This shows a marked reduction in staff overdues which is an encouraging result, but really needs to be taken again at the same time of the year for a more accurate analysis of the statistics (see Annexe No.6).

The list of Methods (solutions) which we brainstormed at the beginning of the project is attached and those problems which have been resolved are marked with an asterisk (see Annexe No.7).

Benefits of Quality Circles

In general the Circle feels that we have been able to tackle problems which may have been longstanding and at first thought may have seemed impossible to solve. It enabled everyone involved with the problems to look at them from different perspectives and approach them in a wholly new light. One of the main benefits to the Library staff has been the improved communications which has resulted, we have been able to meet, some of us for the first time, and exchange views and work problems, making us feel more as part of a team serving one College rather than totally separate libraries.

ANNEXE NO. 1

MATERIALS

REMINDERS IGNORED

METHODS

NO FINES
NO PUNISHMENT
STUDENTS ON PLACEMENT/
 LEAVING
TOO MANY TICKETS FOR STAFF
NO BLACKLISTING
FOLLOW UP INVOICES
REMINDERS IGNORED
SHORT LOANS NOT CHASED UP
STUDENT IDENTITY
STAFF OVERDUES NOT SENT
 OFTEN
CASUAL ISSUE OF TICKETS

BORROWERS

ATTITUDES
STUDENTS ON PLACEMENT/
 LEAVING
STUDENTS FORGET
PASSING BOOKS TO EACH OTHER
STAFF PRIVATE LIBRARIES
REMINDERS ORGNORED

OVERDUE BOOKS

MACHINES

STAMP CLEARER

MANPOWER

LIBRARY STAFF NOT MAKING
 LENGTH OF LOAN CLEAR
SHORT LOANS NOT CHASED UP
DIFFICULTIES IN SENDING
 OVERDUES
STAFF OVERDUES NOT SENT
 OFTEN
CASUAL ISSUE OF TICKETS

OVERDUE BOOKS – CAUSES

A CAUSE AND EFFECT ANALYSIS

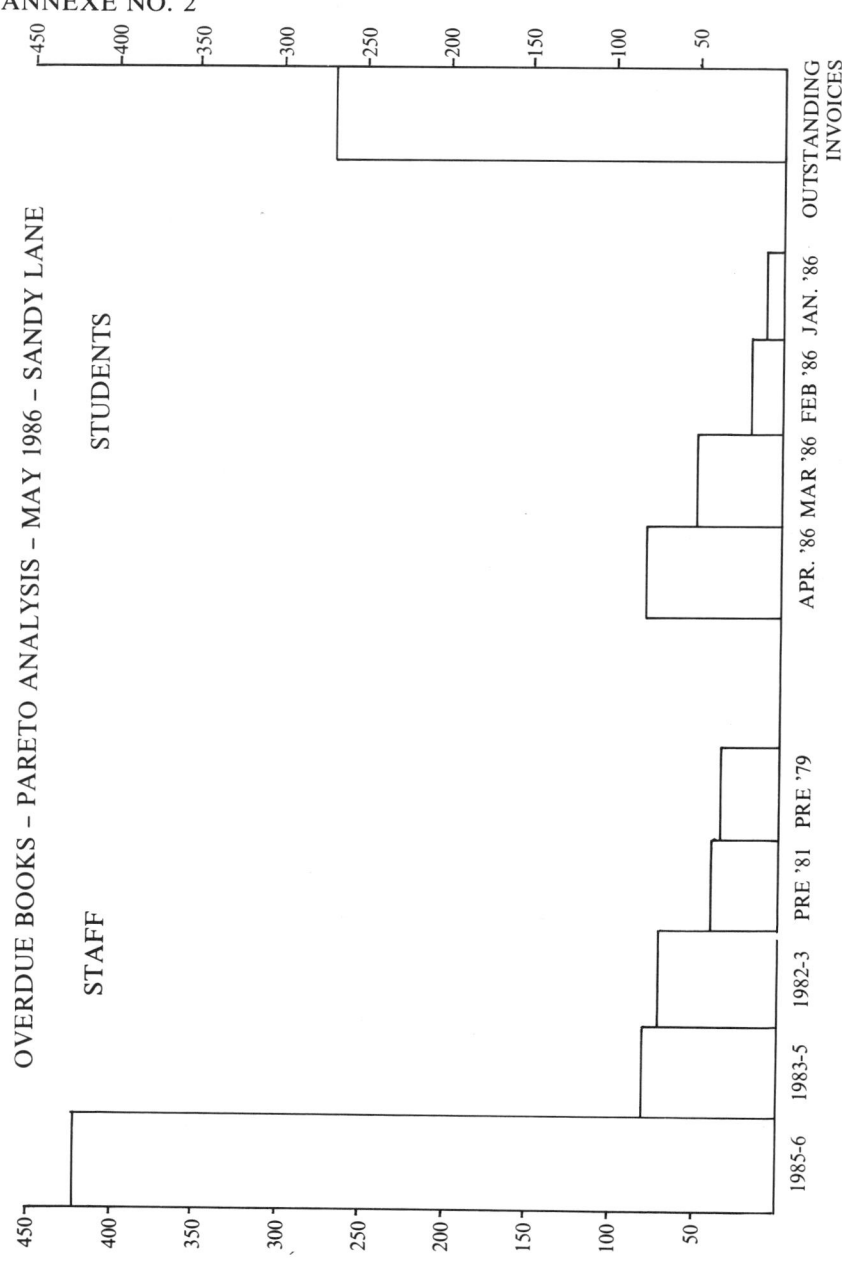

ANNEXE NO. 3

ANY COLLEGE STUDENT (FULL OR PART-TIME) MAY JOIN THE LIBRARY.

Students are issued with up to FOUR tickets.

TICKETS ARE NOT TRANSFERABLE

DO NOT ALLOW ANYONE ELSE TO USE YOUR TICKETS
(You will be held responsible for any books issued in your name)

BOOKS ARE ISSUED FOR 4 WEEKS - PLEASE RETURN THEM PROMPTLY

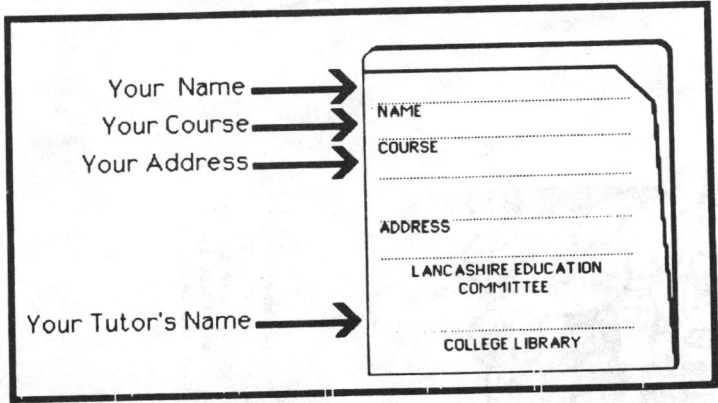

PLEASE SHOW THE LIBRARY STAFF SOME PROOF OF IDENTITY WHEN ASKING FOR TICKETS

ANNEXE 4

This leaflet has been produced by the "Ideas Ad Lib" Quality Circle. This should lead to an improved service for staff and students. Your ideas or constructive criticism are welcomed.

Monday 8th December
Went to College Library this morning – wonderful place. Was amazed to discover that I could borrow up to ten books at any one time! Borrowed "Reindeer herds: breeding and management and "1001 uses for a dead reindeer" to be going on with. Pleased to know I could have them for a month.

Tuesday 9th December
Urgently required to consult a copy of the "Blue Peter Book of sleigh construction and repair". Most put out to find book not on the shelf. Decided to reserve it but was then embarrassed to be informed that it was already issued to me! Look through Times Ed for new job – nothing doing. Bad day all round.

Wednesday 10th December
During search for missing book, came across several others. Had finished with "Beginners guide to sledge acrobatics" but needed to renew "Decorating your family tree" by Princess Michael.

Thursday 11th December
Returned overdue books to Library and renew those still required. Sport "How to improve your memory" and take it out.

Friday 12th December
Have read first two chapters of book, but still not too confident of remembering. Delighted to find that the Library staff will send me reminders every month. Must remember to look in my pigeon hole regularly. Better read rest of book tonight.

Monday 15th December
Several younger elves enquiring about CPVE courses. Having a clear conscience now about library books, feel able to ask Library Staff (in confidence) if they can find out what CPVE meant. Most impressed when they knew without looking it up and provided FEU pamphlet on same. Did not dare ask what FEU meant.

Tuesday 16th December
Called in Staff room – great deal of excitement about my pamphlet, several staff wanting to borrow it from me. Had to insist that they borrowed it from Library when I had finished with it. Made mental note to return it as soon as possible now that I knew people obviously desperate to read it.

Wednesday 17th December
Reserved "Unusual ways to stuff a turkey". Felt sorry for Rudolph, who had today received invoice for book not returned after 3 reminders. Was his nose red! Has had to sell TSB shares! I tried not to look too smug.

Thursday 18th December
In my new-found zeal, encouraged everyone to return or renew their library books.

Friday 19th December
Last day of term! Took out my Christmas reading – "Minsk Spies" by John Le Carré, and "Self-defence for the January Sales".

Decided New Year's Resolutions –

Return or renew books on time.
I won't hog books I don't need.

ANNEXE NO. 5

ANNEXE NO. 6

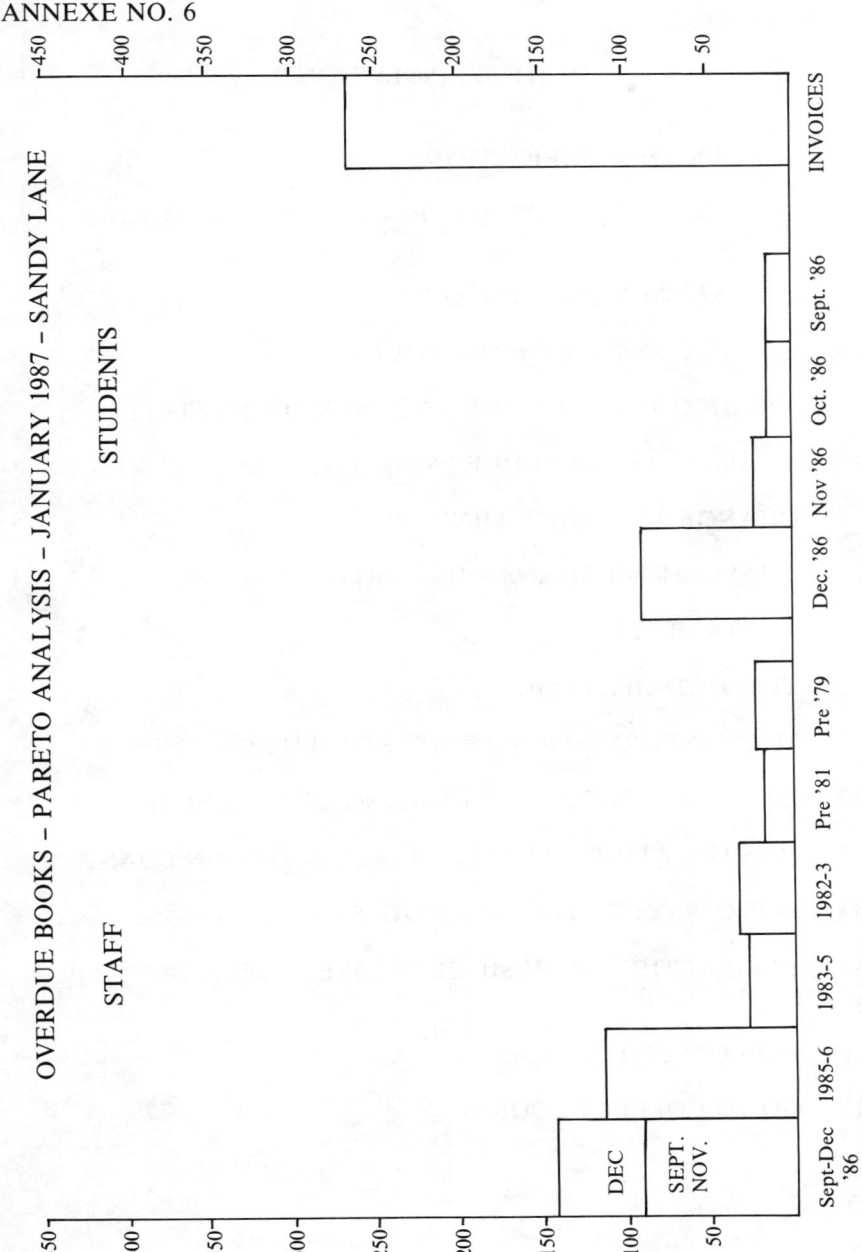

ANNEXE NO. 7

METHODS (SOLUTIONS)

1. STUDENT IDENTIFICATION   *
2. PUNISHING THEM BY STOPPING THEM BORROWING BOOKS
3. ISSUING TICKETS ONCE ONLY   *
4. SPECIFIC SYSTEM OF OVERDUES   *
5. SPECIFIC SYSTEM OF ISSUING TICKETS TO STAFF
6. CHASE STAFF OVERDUES MORE THAN ONCE A YEAR   *
7. CHANGE TYPE OF REMINDERS   *
8. CHASE SHORT LOANS MORE FREQUENTLY   *
9. EXTRA STAFF
10. STAFF CO-OPERATION   *
11. MORE INFORMATION ABOUT STUDENT COURSES
12. IMPROVE METHODS OF CHASING UP STUDENTS   *
13. MONTHLY LIST TO STAFF OF ALL BOOKS ON LOAN
14. PERMISSION TO POST OVERDUES   †
15. TAKE ACTION ON RESIDUE OF OVERDUE BOOKS IN SEPTEMBER   *
16. FOLLOW UP INVOICES   *
17. GO TO COLLECT BOOKS